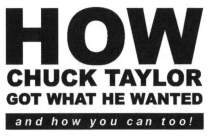

HOW
CHUCK TAYLOR
GOT WHAT HE WANTED

and how you can too!

Third Edition

by

William F. Staats
Professor of Banking and Finance
Louisiana State University

and

E. D. Sledge
President
Consumer Credit Counseling Services
Baton Rouge, Louisiana

Library of Congress Catalog Card Number
00-104210
Published by Credit Counseling Services of Louisiana, Inc.
dba Consumer Credit Counseling Services
615 Chevelle Court
Baton Rouge, Louisiana 70806
225-923-2227

Produced in cooperation with the
Council for Professional Education, Inc.

Printed and Bound in the United States of America

ISBN: 0-9627885-2-X   Price: $14.95

This book is dedicated to all of the responsible young adults who enter the American workforce and marketplace each year.

America's future is in their hands.

Today, more than ever, money and credit play a critical role in everyone's life. Everyone will have some form of income. Learning to make the most of it will ultimately prove more important than the actual amount of that income. For most people, credit will be the tool that most affects how well their income is managed.

ACKNOWLEDGMENTS

The authors would like to express their sincere gratitude to the following persons, organizations, and companies who have been of tremendous help and support in preparing this book.

The CCCS, Baton Rouge, Board of Directors

The past and present board members of this organization have built a solid foundation for credit education, which has become an integral part of the CCCS mission. Without their vision and leadership, CCCS could not play an important role in providing financial responsibility education to our next generation of consumers.

Participating School Systems and Their Officials, Principals, and Free Enterprise Teachers Across the Nation

Recognizing the importance of credit education, our state's educators have supported our initiatives with enthusiasm. We, the authors, can contribute educational tools such as this book, but it is ultimately the teachers and others in the educational system who deliver important information to the students.

George L. Clauer, III—The Law Firm of Seale, Daigle & Ross

Bankruptcy is a very complex law. When the authors needed to get the important issues boiled down to something understandable and not boring, Mr. Clauer came to our aid, providing most of the text for Appendix B. Our sincere thanks go out to Mr. Clauer for his assistance.

Larry G. Johnson, Certified Public Accountant

Every time we write a new edition of this book, the federal tax laws have changed. And every time, we call on Larry Johnson for the help necessary to get the facts straight for Chapter 14. In spite of a demanding workload, Larry is always willing. The authors know about money and credit, but we leave taxes to the experts. Our thanks to Larry, yet again.

Republic Mortgage Insurance Company (RMIC)

RMIC is owed very special thanks and recognition. This company, headquartered in Winston-Salem, North Carolina, has long recognized the need for personal financial literacy, particularly among young people. RMIC, however, has given much more than lip service to help solve the problem. Learning of the previous edition of this book, RMIC stepped up to the plate and purchased over 40,000 copies, donating those books to many schools in seven states. To encourage this, the third edition, the President and CEO of RMIC, Mr. William A. Simpson, agreed to purchase at least another 80,000 books for donation to even more schools. With this, the second printing of the third edition, RMIC has now sponsored over 165,000 copies of the book. Our compliments to Mr. Simpson and RMIC for their commitment to personal financial literacy education.

Sue Israel of CCCS and Linda Rathburn of the Council for Professional Education

And finally, our special thanks to Sue and Linda for their tireless work in editing, illustrating, proofing, and the countless other details involved with the publication of this text.

William F. Staats
E. D. Sledge
Baton Rouge, Louisiana

Table of Contents

Part II—Earning Money and Using Credit

Introduction to the Third Edition

When 'N SYNC comes up with a hit CD, people buy it. They buy it because they like it. Often, people buy all of the copies the recording company has made. In that case, the company makes some more. So it is with books. So it was with the first edition of this book. The demand for the first book was greater than anticipated. A second printing of the first book was ordered and donated to more schools—a total of 11,000 copies.

Next, a second edition was written, with many updates and revisions. Thanks to the generous sponsorship of 50 financial institutions and businesses, 50,000 copies were donated—enough for every high school in Louisiana. By word of mouth, institutions in several other states learned of the book and ordered them for their local schools. Then Republic Mortgage Insurance Company (RMIC), headquartered in Winston-Salem, North Carolina, learned of the book. They sponsored copies for their local schools. Pleased with the results, and knowing that personal financial literacy was widely lacking among young people, they began ordering books for donation to schools in many other cities. In total, more than 140,000 copies, in six printings, have been donated to schools in a number of states, many of them by RMIC. The book was such a success that we decided to write a third edition. You are holding a copy of the third edition.

When we showed the first edition to potential sponsors in 1991, we were absolutely amazed by the remarks we encountered. Many said, "If I had just had a book like this when I was young, I could have avoided so many mistakes!" Such great interest in, and enthusiastic response to, that first edition made us really look forward to writing the second edition. But, this world is changing rapidly. To help you keep pace with it, and to be a successful manager of your financial life, this third edition has been revised to contain many new things you will need to know. As we move into the twenty-first century, we are thrilled to be able to help many more thousands of youth understand a bit of the financial world they are about to face.

Why Read This Book?

"Have you seen the new car Chuck Taylor just bought? That's a sharp car. It's just about as sharp as the one his sister got about a year ago. Those Taylor kids aren't much older than we are. How can they afford those wheels? What do they know that we don't?"

Well, Chuck and his sister must know something because dealers don't just give away cars! What Chuck and his sister know is in this book. That's why this could be one of the most important books you will ever read. This book tells you some financial facts of life and gives them to you straight. It tells you about the real world out there, in terms of your opportunities and your responsibilities.

Now, lots of things are tough out in the real world, and some of them aren't even fair. We may not like that, but that's the way it is. We all have to live in the real world. So, like Chuck and his sister, we are better off knowing exactly how things really are and how things really work in the world we live in.

The authors want you to have a chance to learn these things for a couple of reasons. First, believe it or not, our economic system is full of a lot of good business people. They are sincerely interested in you and your economic future. Second, they know that if you have the chance to learn some economic facts of life and can apply them, you will have a better life—a higher standard of living. Also, the whole economic system will be better off. We're all on this big boat together. The more people who can have a good ride, the better everyone else is. The more people who fail financially, the more the rest of us have to throw life rafts to them. That costs the rest of us money.

Many, if not most, of the readers are going to learn something from this book and be better off. A few will learn a lot. They will use that knowledge all though their lives. Some readers will just browse through this book. When they find out it may not be as entertaining as the latest video, they may just "tune out." Those who tune out now will have some very painful lessons later in life!

In this book, we focus on the way things are. Many of us may not like the way some things are in this world, but that's beside the point. Maybe, someday, you will be motivated to change things for the better. In the meantime, we have to exist. That doesn't mean that we have to conform to all things all the time. However, we all have to play by some important rules that have been in place for a long time. There are certain economic realities that are just as much facts of life as are the facts about sex. We are not telling you how the world ought to be, but how it is.

In 1965 Consumer Credit Counseling Services was organized by the Baton Rouge business community as a non-profit service to provide advice and counseling to people who found themselves over their heads in debt. Back then, counselors at CCCS rarely saw a young person in financial trouble, because young people could not easily borrow money. That's all changed. Now, people are offered the opportunity to establish credit at a much younger age, often in their late teens. Generally, this is a good thing, as many young adults are ready to handle the responsibilities of using credit. But, many others are not. CCCS counselors today often see young people who owe $25,000 or more to creditors. Usually all they have to show for that debt is a car with a mortgage for more than the car is worth! They face several years of sacrifice to pay for their mistakes.

These young people have two things in common: (1) none of them sets out to mess things up on purpose; and (2) all of them ask, "How did this happen to me?" CCCS is able to help most of these young adults. Others may end up in bankruptcy court, branded as a financial failure very early in their lives. Often, that failure could have been avoided had they learned what you have a chance to learn now from this book. Many young people make serious mistakes handling financial decisions and credit responsibility. They just never learned how to make the right decisions regarding money and credit. At a time in their lives when needs (and wants) are the greatest, their income is the smallest. If they do not learn how to use credit wisely, they are likely to get into serious financial trouble that will haunt them for years. These people are not bums, and they aren't stupid either. They just don't know all they need to know. They don't know the things in this book.

By the way, we don't believe that learning has to be boring. We think that a serious subject can still be fun to learn. We've tried to make this book as light and lively as possible. Of course, just like the real world, this book has some tough parts in it.

We show you how Chuck Taylor got much of what he wanted—not everything, but at least some things. We explain the basic economic and financial engine that runs our system. We explain economic wants and desires. We tell you why everyone cannot have everything that he or she desires. Also, we explain who gets to have the things such as cars, nice clothes, a fine house or an apartment, and other things that are produced in our economic system.

You have a chance to learn what you have to know and what you have to do in order to play the game of life successfully—at least that part of life that deals with money. You will get a chance to learn what credit can and cannot do for you, and how to get your credit started. You'll learn why savings are so important—important enough to give up something now for something better later.

As you go through life, this knowledge will help you get more of what you need and want. As a result of this knowledge, you will have the opportunity for a better standard of living. Whoever said that money is not everything in life was right. But money sure helps, and so do the finer things in life that you can have by managing the money you will earn.

Part I

The Basics of Money and the Marketplace

Building a Foundation of Knowledge of the System

*Building a foundation of knowledge is
the key to economic success*

Chapter One

What People Want and
What They Need

Remember when you believed in Santa Claus? You would make a list of things you wanted Santa to bring at Christmas. Chuck Taylor used to have such a list. He said that it was always a long list! There was practically no end to the things Chuck wanted. Most of us were like Chuck. Sometimes we got some of what was on our list, but seldom did we get everything.

Years have passed since most of us found out that the chubby guy in the red suit really didn't exist. Yet we still have a long list of things we want. Take a minute and write down on a piece of paper eight or ten things that you would like to have right now.

Chances are that each person making such a list will have different items on it. More than likely, no two lists will be the same. There may be some things that are on nearly every list. Probably everyone will have at least one thing that doesn't appear on anyone else's list. All of us share some common wants or needs. All of us, however, are different—each of us have some unique wants and needs.

Things such as happiness, health, love, and peace will be on many lists. Probably most of the things on your list are "goods." These are tangible things, such as a car, clothes, a digital sound system, or maybe your own apartment. For some reason, most of us think about goods or possessions when we think of a list of wants or needs. But there is more.

On some lists will be other things, such as medical care, hair styling, good government—these are called "services." They, along with goods, are what make up our economic

standard of living. Services are sometimes more important than goods. We often don't think about services when
we think about our wants and needs—unless our car is in
the shop!

People's wants are unlimited

Necessities of Life

There are some things (whether they appear on our list
or not) that we simply must have. These are "needs"—
called the necessities of life. Examples are food, shelter,
clothes, and medical care. Some might argue that a good
car should rank right up there near the top! A car is a necessity for some people, such as those who use one in their
work or have no way to get to work other than by a private
car. Most teens would argue that they must have a car, but
a lot of them would have a tough time proving it.

Luxuries of Life

At the other end of the scale are "wants" such as luxury
goods and services. Examples of these wants might be a
stay at a fancy resort, a diamond ring, and a membership
in a health club or a spa. Luxury goods and services are
not necessary for survival, and they tend to be expensive.

We can all live quite well without them, but they sure are great to have. They can improve the quality of a person's life, *provided that the person can afford to buy them.*

"In-Between" Goods and Services

Not everything can easily be lumped into one category or the other. Many items fall inbetween needs and wants. However, some could argue that anything that is not a necessity must therefore be a luxury. How each of us views luxuries depends on our own financial condition and our own values. A wealthy student might think that he or she can't get along without steaks or designer jeans. Another student might think that those things were ridiculous luxuries. Many young people in poor, third-world nations would think that school itself was a luxury to dream about.

In the United States, we tend to take our standard of living for granted. The very poorest of us would be seen as very rich by millions of people in the world. Because the more we have the more we want, we often fail to appreciate what we do have. Thanks to our U.S. economic system, we have more opportunities to get more goods and services than most people in the world have. But while most of us *can* have more, it's unlikely that most of us will ever get all we want.

Read on to learn the rules of the game. Chuck Taylor learned these things. As a result, he is making great progress in meeting more of his needs and fulfilling more of his wants.

THINGS TO REMEMBER

Needs are goods and services which everyone must have to live or survive. They are basic necessities.

Wants are those goods and services which people desire to have, but are not necessarily needed for survival. They are luxuries.

There are things that cannot always be accurately classified as either a necessity or a luxury. These are the "in-between" goods and services.

People in the United States enjoy more goods and services than do most of the other people in the world.

Chapter Two

Why Everyone Can't
Have Everything

Even though Chuck is driving around in his new car, the truth is that he really wants a Porsche. That has always been Chuck's dream, and maybe it will be for a long time. Right now Chuck can't handle the eighty "grand" that a Porsche costs! So his desire remains just that—a desire, maybe even a goal. More on goals later.

There are two reasons that most of us have unfulfilled wants on our list. First, we don't have enough money to buy everything we want. Second, there are not enough goods and services in the whole world to satisfy the desires of everyone. Not everyone can have everything he or she wants. Most of us have the potential in life to have a lot more than we have now. Chances are, however, that none of us will have everything we want. Why this is true is explored in the following sections.

Production

In the Old Testament section of the Bible, there is a story that goes something like this. God sent the whole Israelite community in a mass escape from Egypt across the Red Sea and into the desert. Moses was the leader. There wasn't much going on in the desert at the time. No one was trucking in water, and no Red Cross was airlifting supplies. The people complained to Moses, fearing that they were going to starve to death. Then God caused food, called manna, to rain down from the sky. The people had only to pick it up and eat it.

Except for that one instance, throughout human history people have had to produce what they wanted and needed.

Air seems to be freely available; but with pollution today, even clean, healthy air is costing us a price. The car Chuck is enjoying had to be produced. The clothes we are all wearing right now had to be made. The schools had to be built, and the food we eat had to be grown. Somebody made the movies we watch.

Some people, including many politicians, often behave as if just wishing for more goods and services would automatically create them. It just doesn't work that way. For us to have and enjoy goods and services, they must first be produced. If no one is willing to work to produce these things, then they will not be available. That is a basic economic fact of life. Everything has to be produced, and production of everything depends on *factors of production*.

Factors of Production

To produce any good or service, we need five types of things: *labor, capital goods, resources, technology,* and *land*. Even with all of these, we need one more thing— entrepreneurship, which we describe later. Everything that is produced consists of some combination of these factors. In fact, the only thing that makes one good or service different from another is that different types of each of the factors are combined in the production process. This book, your clothes, and your car (if you have one), however different, were each produced by a combination of the five factors of production. In the United States, we are fortunate because we have an abundance of the *factors of production*.

Labor

Labor is one of the most familiar factors of production because we know that most people work. Without labor, everything grinds to a halt. Even highly automated machines cannot function without human labor. First the machines are invented, and then they are manufactured. Then they must be maintained, and finally replaced when they wear out.

There is one overwhelming reason for people to work: work brings reward. That reward is called a paycheck— money! That reward makes it possible for workers to buy goods and services. And for most of us, a sense of accomplishment is another reward we get from working.

Workers are needed to produce goods and services

Production of things such as a house or a work of art requires a lot of labor. Other things, such as notebook paper, can be produced with very little labor. The key point is that some labor is a necessary input for every good or service.

On the job, Chuck Taylor works. Chuck's labor is required to produce something. If Chuck doesn't show up for work, production slows. Chuck and all other workers perform an important function, whatever the job is.

Capital Goods

Labor alone is not enough to produce goods and services. Workers need tools, equipment, and factories to work in. We call these things capital goods. Even in the most primitive economies, workers need capital in order to produce something. For example, the early American Indian hunters needed bows and arrows to hunt meat to eat. Farmers need tractors, truckers need trucks, plumbers need wrenches, steel workers need blast furnaces. The list goes on and on.

Resources

Without raw materials to work with, no goods can be produced. The Indian with the best bow and the most arrows still needed resources in the form of deer and the other wild animals to produce something to eat. Today, we could not produce clothes, cars, or anything else without raw materials.

Resources are natural things that are required in the production of every good or service. Among the common resources are wood, iron ore, oil, cotton, and water. Our world is blessed with abundant, but often abused, resources.

Resources are needed to make goods

Technology

All the labor, capital, and resources in the world would not result in production of any goods or services without technology. "Know-how" is another term for technology. Corning Ware, those bowls in our kitchens, was not produced until we learned how from the U.S. program of space exploration. During the days of the horse and buggy, the resources existed to produce automobiles. But cars could not be made until someone developed the technology for the internal combustion engine. Before the price of autos could be reduced enough for many families to afford them, Henry Ford had to develop the technology of the production line.

It is easy to overlook technology or take it for granted. But we must realize that nothing can be produced without "know-how." Also, to increase the efficiency of production, we must continually improve technology. If you want to increase the value of your labor (so you will receive greater rewards), you must learn new things and improve your skills especially with computers. That way, you can produce more and better things and your labor will be worth more. You will get to enjoy more goods and services.

Technical skills are needed to produce goods and services

Land

Of course, we need a place where we can bring together the first four factors of production. That place is land. However, it could be on the sea as in the case of a floating fish factory. Maybe one day it will be in the form of an orbiting space station! But even if the sea and space are used in production, we still need some old fashioned land. We need a place for the ships to dock as well as a place to launch and land the spaceships. Land, then, is a factor of production.

Land is one of the factors of production

Entrepreneurship

This word is hard to pronounce. Try "on-trey-pray-newer-ship." What it means is the creative act of putting together the five factors of production. You see, we can have lots of land, labor, capital, resources, and technology. But until someone takes the initiative to put them all together and organizes the activity, we will have no production. People who do that are called entrepreneurs. Business owners and managers often are entrepreneurs. The richest man in the world, Bill Gates, is an entrepreneur.

Wants and Scarcity

We need very little to exist. Food, water, air, shelter, and of course, love and attention from other people are necessary. But everyone wants more than just a basic existence. In fact, if people were to list everything they really wanted, some would never stop writing.

Many or most of our wants will never be satisfied because the factors of production are limited. There is only so much labor available, so much capital, so many resources, and so much technology. Therefore, there is a limit as to how much can be produced in, say, a given year. We have unlimited wants, but limited resources to produce those things. However, as people become more educated, labor becomes more productive. Resources can be used more efficiently as technology is advanced. So, over time we can increase the rate of growth in production of goods and services. Better education results in a better standard of living for working people.

How Much Gets Produced?

The answer to the above question should be simple. We produce all we can. But it really doesn't work that way. People may choose to produce less than the greatest amount possible. People trade off labor for vacation. Sometimes we leave some lands unspoiled rather than use the resources from them. These are only two examples that show that we often produce less than the greatest possible amount of goods and services.

We may choose to limit production in many ways, but we cannot produce more than the *factors of production* will allow. It has been estimated that the factors of production increase by roughly five percent a year. New natural resources are discovered, land is developed and made usable, labor becomes more productive, and technology is improved. This means the maximum amount of goods and services that can be produced can expand by only that same five percent each year. Despite what some politicians seem to preach, not everyone can have everything he or she wants!

Because things are scarce, they have value. The more scarce something is, the more value it has. If gold could be found everywhere, jewelry would be cheaper. Perhaps, then, we would not want it as much. The concept of scarcity and value is a simple one, but very important. Understanding this concept helps us to understand many other economic facts of life.

What Gets Produced?

Because of the limits on total production in the economy, we have to decide what specific goods and services get produced. In socialistic or communistic countries, government officials decide what will be produced. A relatively small group of people make the decisions. In a market economy, such as ours, *we* decide what gets produced. Did you know that? We buy what we decide we need and want the most. Therefore, that's what companies will make.

Each of us, by our actions in the marketplace, helps decide what goods and services are produced. When we quit buying buggy whips for horse carriages, factors of production were no longer channeled to making that product. When we started wanting and buying the new cellular telephones, more labor, capital, resources, and technology were directed toward increased production of that product. People obviously want a cure for cancer and for AIDS. Factors of production are being channeled toward finding those cures.

As you and Chuck and I spend money, we are *voting in the market* for what we want produced. The economy responds to that spending by using the factors of production to produce the things we want.

But remember, there are limits of production in the short-run. If our demand for a product increases faster than the factors of production, prices will go up. However, if one or more of the factors of production are increased (especially technology), prices will go down. For example, good quality TVs and VCRs are cheaper today than they were 10 years ago largely because of the advances in technology.

Chuck Taylor's new car is a combination of the factors of production. Land, labor, capital goods, resources, and technology were combined and resulted in a car. The steel that went into Chuck's car could not also be used to make another product. The same is true for the other factors of production.

In spending money to buy that car, Chuck was telling business people that he wanted those factors of production to go into the automobile. That is how each of us helps to decide what gets produced. That is also why we Americans have the highest standard of living in the world. That's also why we enjoy the greatest selection of goods and services that have ever been available in the history of the world.

Increased technology reduces the cost of goods and services

THINGS TO REMEMBER

The production of goods and services is dependent upon five factors of production: *land, labor, capital goods, resources,* and *technology.*

Entrepreneurship is the process of combining factors of production so that goods and services can be produced.

The supply of the factors of production can be increased within limits. If production is increased through better productivity and wiser use of resources, we are all better off.

There are not enough resources available for all of us to get everything we desire.

Paychecks or money is the reward to people for providing the labor necessary to produce goods and services.

What gets produced in the marketplace in the U.S. is decided mainly as a result of what the people want. This is evidenced by what the people are most willing to spend their money on.

Chapter Three

Who Gets What Is Produced?

A lot of people would like to have Chuck Taylor's new car. In fact, some people may think that it's just not fair that they don't have one like it. When some people see others who have more goods and services than they have, they cry "foul."

Sure, it would be great if everyone had a new car and everything else he or she wanted! But we pointed out in the last chapter that the economy simply cannot produce enough goods and services to satisfy everybody's wants. So, who gets what is produced? That's one of the hottest questions in our society. We find the answers in this part of the book.

How the System Works

In the United States, most goods and services go to the people who have earned the money to purchase them. People like Chuck who work provide labor. As a reward for contributing to production, they get paychecks. Those paychecks and the money that they represent can be used to buy goods and services. And if people are smart, they stash a little of their income away for a rainy day so that they can spend it when emergencies or opportunities come up later. So, the money people receive for working is the incentive for them to provide labor. Money is why most people work.

Some of our money is taxed away from workers and put into government welfare programs. This helps provide at least a minimum level of living for those who are unable to participate in the economic process. Some people cannot work because of some type of mental or physical impairment. Surely we have to take care of the people who would work if they were able. However, the productive portion of our society has limitations on how much of what it produces can be directed to a non-productive segment.

Without labor, as we saw earlier, there can be no production. Without production, there can be no goods and services. A system of rewards promises each of us that if we provide the labor needed to produce things, we can get more of what we want. If we work, we can get at least some of what is produced. Generally speaking, the more and better we work, the more we get.

Chuck used income from his part-time job to buy his car

Chuck's part-time job provided him with disposable income. Disposable income is income in excess of that required for necessities. At first, Chuck saved that disposable income toward a down payment on his car. When he had enough savings to meet that goal, he bought the car. Then he began directing his income to the monthly payments. In the meantime, some of his friends were just hanging around. Now, they envy his car and wish they had one too.

Chuck didn't make a lot of money when he first started on his job a few years ago. In fact, sometimes he wondered if it was worth it. But he kept working. In the process, he learned more about his job and how to be of more value to his employer. As his value increased, so did his pay. He's making even more now. And when he finishes his education, he's got a chance at earning some "big bucks."

It's a fact of life that not everybody is paid the same for the same hours of work. The value of labor depends on many things. There is a demand for people who have skills, knowledge, and experience. They will earn more than someone who is unskilled, undereducated, and inexperienced. Generally speaking, the more that someone can contribute to the economy, the more he or she will get out of it. That's the reward system.

Let's face it. Some people are a bit lazy. Many of them would like to take two six-month vacations each year! But if they don't work, they don't contribute anything to the production of goods and services. Hence, they don't deserve to have any of the goods and services that are produced by those who do work. Don't think for a minute that Chuck worked hard to see someone else get his new car. Would you? In this country, each person has the choice *not* to work. But those who choose not to work should have no claim on the goods and services that the rest of us work to produce.

The Market

There is a market for just about everything. Every good and service can be bought and sold. The "market" does not mean just a place where buying and selling take place. The term "market" also describes how people behave in an economic way. We need to understand this market, because we are all a part of it. We are all actively buying and selling things. For example, we sell our labor when we work. In our country, the market is the main way we answer the question, "Who gets what is produced?" By the way, the market is also the way we decide *what* gets produced and *how* those things are produced. Let's check that out.

When Chuck bought his new car, he sent a message to the market. That message said, "Make more cars. Allocate more factors of production to automobiles." Here is how that works. When demand for a particular good or service increases, the price of that item goes up in relation to the prices of other goods and services. In turn, that higher price attracts more of the factors of production. For example, if the *demand* for cars increases, the company making the cars needs more workers. That will tend to increase wages to attract additional workers. The same thing happens to the other factors of production: resources, capital goods, technology, and land.

When people stopped buying as many tapes and started buying more compact discs, factors of production shifted to meet the new demand. That increased the supply of compact discs. This was the result of our votes in the marketplace.

Supply and Demand

The price, or value, of each factor of production, as well as the value of every good or service, is determined by two things: supply and demand. Here is a general rule that always works no matter what the good or service is. The greater the supply relative to demand, the lower the price will be. The opposite is also true. If demand for some good or service increases and supply does not, the price will rise.

Price

In the late 1990s, fast food stores like Burger King and McDonald's in parts of the northeastern U.S. were advertising for workers. The pay was around nine dollars an hour! That's a fairly high wage for jobs which don't require much skill and are available to high school students. Why was that pay so high? Well, there were more of those jobs available than there were workers willing to do that work. In other words, demand exceeded supply, so the price of labor went up. We call the price of labor "wages."

In the early 1970s, the price of a gallon of gasoline was around 30 cents. Look at the price now. It is now around a dollar and a quarter a gallon. Here's what happened.

In 1974, the Arab nations that produce a very large part of the world's crude oil stopped selling that oil for a while. They wanted to drive the price up. It worked. By sharply reducing the supply of oil, from which gasoline is made, the price of gas increased. Later in the seventies, trouble in Iran caused a further decrease in the supply. The result was still higher prices at the pump.

During the late eighties, there no longer seemed to be a threat to the supply of oil. The price of oil dropped somewhat.

In 1990, the invasion of Kuwait by Iraq threatened the supply of crude oil. The immediate result was that the price of gasoline soared again. As soon as the U.S. and its allies forced Iraqi troops back where they belonged, the supply of oil was again secured and the market settled down.

Oil shortages mean higher prices at the gas pump

On the demand side, we were producing and driving more cars. The population was growing; so, people bought more gasoline. Growing demand, then, also helped to push up the price of a gallon of gasoline.

Simply stated, the relationship of the supply of something together with the demand for that good or service determines the price.

Quantity

Supply and demand determine the amount of any good or service that is produced in our economy. At every price, say for gasoline, there is some amount that we will buy. As the price goes up, we buy less. As the price goes down, we buy more. That is called the "Law of Demand." That's not a law passed by Congress. It's a true statement about the market and how we behave with respect to price. No Congress or legislature can repeal the "Law of Demand." As the price of a good or service goes up, people who supply that good or service will put more on the market. At a lower price, they will put less on the market. Consumers generally will buy more of anything at a lower price, and less at a higher price.

That's how the market system works. Our economic activity is based on the market system. It works better than any other type of economic system in the world. People throughout history have tried other ways of deciding what should be produced, how to set the price, and who should get what is produced. In the entire history of the world, no other system has worked as well as ours. In fact, communist nations such as Russia and China are moving toward the market system. They have accepted the fact that their old systems simply don't work as well as ours. Our system isn't perfect, but it is the best yet! It puts more goods and services into the hands of more people than any other system we know.

Who Gets What Is Produced?

People who have money, or the opportunity to use credit, get what is produced. It's just that simple! The more money and income a person has, the more he or she can buy.

Remember, Chuck got what he wanted because he had the income from his job and, thus, the opportunity to use credit. Others with no money or credit may have wanted that car just as much as Chuck did. It is possible they may have needed it more. But Chuck was productive, and he got it.

Generally, people who work to help produce goods and services are the ones who can afford to buy. It's a fact that some people get paid more than others for their work. Let's see why that is.

There is a demand for and a supply of labor, as we stated in the previous pages. If you are able to provide the kind of labor that (1) is more in demand and (2) has relatively fewer workers competing for that kind of work, your earnings will be higher. That's because of the supply and demand that we explained earlier. Check out Shaquille O'Neal and the amount of money he earns.

Hard work is rewarded in the marketplace

Because a limited number of people have a good education, good skills, and useful knowledge, the supply of such workers is relatively scarce. The demand, however, for these people is great. The result is a higher wage rate. Those people are able to contribute more to the production of goods and services. Therefore, they are rewarded by the market system with higher pay. Those are the folks with more money and credit. They get to buy more of what is produced.

THINGS TO REMEMBER

In the U.S. economy, people decide what gets produced. They "vote" in the marketplace by buying goods and services.

The supply of and demand for goods and services (including labor) determines the market price.

People who have the most valuable knowledge and skills in the work force receive a greater proportion of the goods and services produced.

As demand for a good or service increases, the price of that good or service will increase unless supply can be increased.

If supply increases without an increase in demand, the price will drop.

People who work get the money and the credit which they can use to buy goods and services in the market.

Chapter Four

Who Are the Players that Win?

In this country's economic system, we are free to participate in the production of goods and services. In fact, if we really want any of those things on our want list, we have to play the game. Yes, life is serious, but it can be compared to a game. Those who prepare well and play to win usually are the winners. Some people cannot play because they are physically or mentally impaired. Their handicap is beyond their control. That's why those of us more fortunate support them through private charitable organizations and through government welfare programs.

Chuck had the game figured out. He had help. He had a chance to learn from some mistakes his older sister made. She had dropped out of high school with only a year to go. "Just got bummed out on school," she said. She had a tough time. No one would hire her for a good job with a chance for real advancement. She scratched out a few bucks here and there. She did it the hard way and without much reward. It was a real drag. She had little income and couldn't buy new clothes or many of the other things she needed, let alone wanted. Without the good pay that a decent job provides, she just didn't get to play.

Chuck saw his sister's problems, and he is sticking it out in school. In fact, he has worked part-time all through high school and college. By the way, his sister got her act together and went back to finish school. It was a lot harder, but by then she was just a little bit wiser. Now she has a job with a real future and is making good money.

*A good education can help you make
today's dreams a reality tomorrow*

What Is Money?

We can make a good case that love makes the world go around. There is love for our family, for ourselves and our friends, for our country, for the Supreme Being. Maybe love is the basic thing in life, but money is a close second. Let's face it—money is important.

Most people really don't understand exactly what money is and all that money does even though they are around it most of the time. A lot of us think of money as nickels, dimes, quarters, and the "folding stuff." But coin and currency, as those things are called, make up only a little of our supply of money. Other things also serve as money.

If we want to define money, we must say that money is anything that is generally accepted as performing the *functions of money.* That may sound a little fuzzy, but that is what money is. So, money is anything people will accept as performing those things we expect money to do for us.

Weird things have been accepted as money in some societies. For example, in one of the South Pacific island societies, people used belts made of feathers from red birds which lived on the islands. Other strange types of money used in the past include rocks, beads, fur pelts from animals—and yes, even something called gold.

Some of these things that perform the functions of money today include checking accounts, travelers checks, savings accounts, and other things. All of these, along with coin and currency, are generally accepted as performing the functions of money.

The Functions of Money

Money performs important functions for us individually and for the whole economy. We need to understand these functions so that we can use money properly.

Medium of Exchange

The most obvious function of money is as a *medium of exchange*. That means that we can use money to buy goods such as a new computer, an EarlyDawn CD, a pair of shoes, or a hamburger. Also, we use money to buy services, such as a haircut or car repairs. We exchange money for a service or a product. That's its function as a medium of exchange.

Store of Value

Money does more than allow us to buy things. Most of us have saved money. In fact, if you have money in your purse or pocket right now, you have saved money if only for just a little while. Perhaps you are saving money until you get enough together to buy a new portable CD player. So, money serves as a *store of value*. In other words, we don't have to run out and exchange money for goods or services the moment we get it. Instead, we can hold it as a power to buy something in the future. This is simply called *saving*. When we are ready at sometime in the future, we can exchange the cash or part of our checking account or savings account balance for the goods or services for which we have been saving. In this way money serves as a store of value.

In effect, money represents a claim check. We can use it at any time. In the meantime, the money is acting as a storehouse of purchasing power. The function as a store of value is a pretty handy thing.

Unit of Measurement

Money also serves as a *measure of value*. That's a fancy term for a measuring stick. We can use the measure of value to gauge incomes, prices, wealth, and things like that. When we compare a Chevy to a Porsche, we know one costs, say, four times as much as the other. Also, we may know someone who earns twice as much income as another person. Money allows us to express those different values in a very precise way. So money serves as a measure of value.

Where Does Money Come From?

Chuck used to think that there was a fixed amount of money in the country. When one person received it, someone else had to give it up. Well, that's only partially true.

Chuck has worked part-time after school and on Saturdays. He noticed that when he got paid, he had that money and his boss no longer had it. He also noticed that later on Saturday nights, he no longer had all of the money. Someone else had the money he spent. It seemed to Chuck that the same amount of money was simply changing hands as people bought and sold goods and services.

Only later did Chuck learn that the amount of money in the country is not fixed. Rather, it gets larger as the need arises and smaller when the need is over. The supply of money in the U.S. expands and contracts as needed. How that works is beyond the scope of this book. We can tell you that something called the *Federal Reserve System* controls the ability of commercial banks to make loans to business firms as well as to us. In the simplest of terms, as loans are made by banks, the nation's money supply increases. As those loans are repaid, the money supply shrinks. While there is more to it than that, this really happens. It is not all that complicated.

Why All of Us Can't Have All the Money We Want

If money is created when banks make loans, why can't we just require banks to lend money to everybody who needs some? Then we could have all we need! Unfortunately, that won't work. Here is why.

First of all, money by itself doesn't do anything for us. We can't eat it, nor can we wear it. It really has no value other than what can be bought with it. Money by itself does not determine our standard of living. Instead, it is the amount of goods and services over which we have control that determines our standard of living. Money is only the means that each of us uses to acquire those things that, in turn, determine our standard of living.

The problem is that there is a limited quantity of desirable things in this country and in all of the world. No matter what the politicians say or do, they cannot increase the supply of goods and services being produced. Remember the discussion of factors of production in Chapter 2?

Goods and services are scarce. The reason is that everything we want is a combination of resources and there are limits to the resources available. We just cannot produce everything we want. There simply is not enough labor, resources, capital goods, land, or technology.

To get votes, some politicians often promise to give people more money. Well, let's look at what would happen to our standard of living if the government gave every person in the country a million dollars!

Let's pretend that some politician made the rounds last night while we were all asleep. Let's say he or she dropped a suitcase with a million dollars at everybody's door. This morning, each of us woke up, and there it was. Wow! What would be the first thing you would do?

How would you like a million bucks?

If you were in school, you would probably "skip." But that wouldn't have mattered, because the school would be empty. Remember, everybody else got a million bucks also! Even the teachers. So, they probably would skip, too!

Remember that want list? High up on my list would be a new car. So I go down to the dealer with my suitcase full of money to buy the model I've been wanting. Boy, would I be excited! But what would I find when I got there? I would find a long line of people, each hugging a suitcase full of cash. What could have happened in just a few hours is that suddenly the demand for cars, boats, houses, and everything else skyrocketed. But the supply did not. All of a sudden, I realize that while the Santa Claus politician was running all over delivering suitcases full of money, there were no little elves busy in the factories making things overnight.

So here I am at the dealership. Maybe that's you right ahead of me in the long line. What do you think is about to happen? Some guy back in the line is going to see that the dealer will run out of cars. So he shouts to a salesman waiting on somebody else, "Hey, I'll give you $10,000 over sticker for that red one!" Another guy with his eye on the red one hollers, "I'll give you $20,000 over!" In about 10 seconds, everybody in line is bidding up the price of the cars. Each person has plenty of cash, but the cars are scarce.

Don't forget, the same thing is happening all over town and all over the country. At every car dealership, boat place, furniture store, shopping mall, and everywhere else people have suitcases full of money. Every kid who's been wanting to get his own apartment is out on the street looking. But only the early birds would get the worm, because there are only just so many goods and services available. And guess what's happening to prices?

Literally, within minutes that morning, the price of everything in the country would have gone out of sight. It would probably take more than a million bucks to buy that car! Everyone would be worse off because the price of everything would be sky-high. That afternoon, when you got hungry, a hamburger would probably cost $100, if you could find one. Don't forget, very few workers showed up for work. The production of goods and services ground to a screeching halt.

The only part of this story that's a fairy tale is everyone getting the million dollars. If that would have happened, the results we described would be true. Too much money chasing too few goods drives prices up. That is called inflation.

Having more money does not necessarily mean that we are better off. Our standard of living depends not on how much money we have, but rather it depends on the amount of goods and services we can buy with the money we have.

It's true that if the amount of money *you* have increases faster than the amount *other* people have, you will be better off. One of your real-world challenges is to learn how to earn more so you can be worth more. Another, and very important, challenge is to learn how to use intelligently what you do earn. If you can earn more and use your money wisely, you are going to have a higher standard of living.

From this book you will be able to learn about some of the things that you can do to play the game and to be a winner. You need to learn how to earn a good income, how to use credit wisely, and how to manage your finances well. Then you can play the game as well as Chuck, or maybe even better.

THINGS TO REMEMBER

Money can be anything that will perform the functions of money.

The functions of money are a *medium of exchange*, a *store of value*, and a *measure of value*.

Too much money in the economy causes inflation—that is, the price of goods and services increases.

It is not the number of dollars you have or earn that is important; rather, it is the amount of goods and services you can buy with the money you have that affects your standard of living.

Managing the money you do earn wisely is as important as earning money in the first place.

Chapter Five

Setting Goals, Making Choices, and Establishing Priorities

Almost everybody wants to be richer. Most people are motivated to earn more, to achieve an ever-higher standard of living. For some, however, money seems to hold little attraction. They are motivated by totally different things, and there's nothing wrong with that.

How do people accumulate wealth? A few seem to be born with a silver spoon in their mouth and to get everything handed to them on a platter. At least it seems like that to the rest of us. Usually, people who get ahead in life are able to do so because they have learned to set goals and work to attain them. This goes for athletic activities, financial well-being, and all other aspects of life.

We're not going to tell you to set your sights on being president of the United States. We're not even going to tell you that you should set the goal of becoming rich. If you want either (or both) of these goals, you had better read and learn a lot more than what is in this book.

We can tell you to set your sights on something worthwhile. Then go for it! That's what goal setting is all about. Your goal can be to be rich, to be happily married, to succeed in a career, or to tour the world. Most people have many goals; a few others, unfortunately, don't have any.

Goals
Some people never set goals. They just wander along through life, waiting for whatever comes along. There may be nothing wrong with this, but let's hope these people aren't waiting for good things to happen to them. A lot of

people who don't set goals tend to be failure-prone and don't expect much out of life. It's not likely that you are this type of person, or you wouldn't have read this far in this book.

Another group of people set wildly unrealistic goals. They set themselves up for a failure or disappointment because they have set their sights too high. Of course, being ambitious is one of the keys to accomplishment. But patience and good judgment are just as important.

Careful planning leads to success in whatever we do

Just setting your sights on something isn't going to make it happen. You must have a workable plan. And, you have to carry out that plan. A ladder without steps is useless. Even if it leaned against a strong tree, you couldn't climb it. This is the secret of smart goal setting. Decide what you want, then build a ladder with steps that will get you there.

Your Plan

A simple but effective trick in achieving your big goals is to identify and set intermediate sub-goals or steps. Those steps must be designed like the steps on a ladder leading straight to where or what you want to be. Let's say you want a new car like Chuck's. You can't simply say your goal is to have a new car and expect it to fall out of the sky. Wanting isn't enough! You must have a plan with several intermediate steps. The first step would be to get a job to earn money. The next step is to develop a savings habit so you could make a down payment. That requires self-discipline and budgeting, *and* doing without some other, perhaps less important, things so you don't spend all your earnings. The third step is to establish your credit if you haven't already. Building your earning power and demonstrating your ability to save are the building blocks to establishing credit.

Needless to say, there has to be some common sense to your plan. It has to be realistic, or you set yourself up for disappointment. Let's say that right now you don't have much savings, nor do you have a large income. But you want a Ferrari. No amount of goal setting will help you to pull that off anytime soon. Maybe your first goal should be to get a used car. After all, a clean used set of wheels would beat bumming rides. Intelligent and careful shopping can almost always result in finding good used transportation for very little money. Notice we said transportation. We didn't say the car of your dreams. But that first used car can help lead to a nicer one later on.

Just about everything in life worth having has to be worked for in one way or another. A happy marriage, or just a good relationship with another person, doesn't just happen accidentally. Success in a career rarely falls in anyone's lap. Owning a nice home one day won't happen just because you want it to. All of these things require goal setting and a plan to make them happen. Then you must have the determination to make your plan work.

Choices

No one gets everything he or she wants. We must choose some things over others. In fact, all through life we are faced with choices. We can choose to stay in bed or get up and see what challenges and opportunities the day brings us. Making choices is related to goal setting. We have to decide what we want the most. This is a process of setting priorities—deciding what is most important. Something always has to be sacrificed in order to get something else. No two people always have exactly the same priorities.

If you want a good education, say a college degree, then you usually have to put off a full-time job. But the reward for getting that degree usually is a lifetime of higher earnings and the potential of a better career path. Saving the down payment for a car means not spending some money on other things along the way. If you want a truly rich and rewarding relationship with someone, that also means sacrificing and not being selfish. This is true whether that person is one of your parents, a brother or sister, or a friend of the opposite sex.

There can be a hidden trap in making choices. Sometimes we make choices without really knowing what we are doing. We commit ourselves to things without realizing what we have done. Sometimes we accidentally or carelessly make the most important choices. A simple example is impulse buying. Maybe you have a little extra money, and you're in the mall one day. You went for a pair of shorts, but before you knew it, you spent more than a hundred bucks for a new pair of fancy athletic shoes. And, you bought the shorts. The point is that now you no longer have the choice of what to do with that hundred bucks. You already made it.

A far more serious example could be education. There are too many people who dropped out of high school. At the time, they probably had no plan for success, no goals for achievement. School seemed like a drag. So they dropped out. They made a serious choice in life without realizing the consequences. Later, when things got tough and they couldn't find a good job, they realized the mistake. This happened to Chuck's sister. But unlike most dropouts, Chuck's sister had the intelligence, and the courage, to go back to school.

The bottom line is that successful and happy people do not get that way by accident. They set goals, make choices, and establish priorities in everything they do. Not just in how they spend their money or what kind of car they buy, but in *everything* they do. When they set goals, they strive to achieve them. When they make choices, they do so after carefully considering the options. And they think about the consequences of each choice. When they establish priorities, they are often making choices in their goals.

One thing more—nobody gets out of this life without making mistakes. Some are minor, but many are major ones. What sets some people apart from others is that they see and admit the mistakes they make and learn from them. Then they back up and, using the lessons they have learned, go in another direction. The next time they run into one of life's problems, they are wiser.

As you read further in this book, you are going to learn about how to make yourself of value in a job, what credit is all about, and how to establish and use your credit. We hope you see how the lessons in this chapter will affect you and your life in the future.

THINGS TO REMEMBER

Usually, people who get ahead in life are able to do so because they have learned to set goals and work to attain them.

Have a workable plan to achieve the goals you do set. Do not set unrealistic goals.

No one gets everything he or she wants. We must choose some things over others.

Sometimes we make choices without realizing it. A failure to recognize choices when they present themselves can be a serious trap.

Everyone makes mistakes. Some people recognize and admit mistakes and can learn from them. Others do not, and repeat them.

Part II

Earning Money and Using Credit

Chapter Six

How You Get Money

We all know how people get money. They either earn it, borrow it, steal it, or someone gives it to them. There are only a few who try to steal it, and all of them regret it when they have to pay their dues in jail. So let's leave out the stupid thief, and let's leave out the lucky person who gets money as a gift. That only leaves two ways for you to get money. In this chapter, we tell you some key things to help you earn more money and borrow wisely. In fact, we tell you just what Chuck did, because he's on the right track to a good life.

The only legitimate way to get money is to earn it by working for someone else, by owning your own business, or by receiving returns on investments such as savings. You can also borrow money, but it has to be paid back.

Earning Money

Today, if you are a student in school, you may not be working. But your turn will be here before you know it, and you will be in the market for either a part-time or a full-time job. If you are already working, you are beginning to experience some of what we are talking about. Even if you've been working for just a short while, you've learned that it's a big world out there. And if you want to get ahead, there's a lot more you need to learn.

What It Takes to Get a Job

Do you remember these two factors of production, labor and technology? To get a job, these two factors directly apply to each of us. We must be willing to work (to provide the labor), and we need some knowledge or know-how (technology). Generally speaking, the more you know, the better the jobs available to you.

Skilled labor is in high demand

As we mentioned, Chuck's sister dropped out of school before getting her diploma. The result was that she had limited skills. The only jobs she could get didn't pay much. With only a little knowledge, she couldn't make much of a contribution to the economy; so her reward in terms of pay was very small. Finally, she did go back and finish school. Then she was able to get out of the low-pay trap.

Today, many people entering the job market have college degrees. Competition for good jobs can be tough, especially for someone who does not have much knowledge or training. To get a decent job, you need at least a high school diploma unless you like the idea of slinging hamburgers all of your life. A lot of people have made it big without a college degree. They worked hard. Along the road of success they learned how to be of value. That's what it's all about—learning to be of value. A college degree can help pave the road, but even having five degrees is a waste unless a person is willing to work hard.

When competing for that first real job, it helps a lot to have had part-time work experience. This is true whether you have to go to work right out of high school or after finishing college. Working part-time during school teaches you a lot, and it tells the prospective employer that you know what work is all about.

Chuck's part-time job plus his education helped him land a very good job. It also taught Chuck the importance of:

- showing up for work and showing up on time;

- being neat and dressed for the job;

- working with and getting along with other people;

- being able to produce and be of value; and

- managing time and money wisely and effectively.

Getting to work on time is basic. An employer must be able to count on workers being there and being on time. A poor record of tardiness or absenteeism can cost an otherwise good employee a promotion, and worse, his or her job.

Wearing the proper clothes on the job is important. It is a reflection of maturity and responsibility. Every employee is a representative of his or her employer, and the worker's appearance is important.

More than one person has lost his or her job because he or she could not get along with others. Not being able to get along with others is also an indication of immaturity and irresponsibility. An employer cannot be expected to tolerate this type of problem in the work place.

Productivity, along with all the other necessary traits, is the result of working hard and working smart. It is why people are paid for their labor and their knowledge. Chuck learned quickly to be of value to his employer.

For Chuck, working and being productive meant managing his time well. This trait carried over to all other aspects of Chuck's life, including managing his money well. That's why he was able to save his down payment for the car. That's also why he is always able to make his payments on time.

There is something else important about getting a job and getting ahead. That is the simple habit of looking a person in the eye when talking to him or her. Eye contact is important whether you are applying for a job or just making a good impression on someone. Even if a person is well-dressed, intelligent, and skilled, he or she cannot make a good impression without eye contact. And don't forget to smile and to be polite!

What It Takes to Keep a Job

Getting a job is just the first step. You have to keep it. People can lose jobs for a lot of reasons. These are four main ones:

- they do something dishonest;
- they are not responsible or reliable;
- they are simply not worth what they are paid; or
- the company gets into financial trouble.

The first reason is easy to understand. An employer is not going to tolerate dishonesty, whether it's stealing or lying.

Being responsible and reliable—well, that's not so clear all the time. Some people are able to fool themselves. They convince themselves that they are responsible when their behavior says they are not. We often like to blame others when we mess up. If you fail an exam, it's easy to say, "The teacher didn't teach me that." Well, a teacher cannot teach you anything; all he or she can do is help you to learn. It's the same on the job. We can blame the boss or other workers for our mistakes. We can blame the traffic when we are late. But the bottom line is that we are responsible for what we do—or don't do.

In the very first part of this book, we said we were going to tell it like it is. We said that a lot of things are not fair—or at least they don't seem to be. This business of being paid what you are worth is a perfect example. There is probably no such thing as people being paid exactly what they are worth. We suspect that two conditions about pay exist in the marketplace. Some people are overpaid, and some are underpaid. Those who are overpaid are in trouble. Sooner or later, their jobs will be gone. Perhaps the safest position to be in is to be worth more than you are paid. That way you have no place to go but up!

Learning never stops

How to Grow In a Job

Some people think the learning process stops when they get out of school. This is not true! Everyone is always learning, or at least they should be. The trick is to take advantage of the constant opportunities for learning and put what you learn to work. That way you are always improving, always growing. And your value in the job increases.

Chuck learned that quickly. He reads and keeps up with what is going on in the world. He found a couple of business magazines that focus on his type of work. He knows that if he wants to earn more, he must be worth more. He is always trying to increase his know-how. Chuck constantly increases his value to his job as he increases his knowledge in general. One day he may want to change jobs, and he knows he has to be ready.

Earning Money—Working for Yourself

Working for another person isn't the only way to earn money. While it may be the best way for many people, lots of others make it big on their own as entrepreneurs. It's not easy starting and running your own business. In fact, a lot of people who have big ideas about running their own business wind up broke. Generally, these are the dreamers looking for the easy way, and those who were not prepared. A lot of them wouldn't do well in a regular job either.

Most of us start out working for someone else—someone who is a successful business person. There is the opportunity to learn and earn—and to save money. Also, working in a job creates an environment for meeting people and building a good reputation. It takes all of these things for success.

To be successful in your own business, you have to have the technology—the know-how. To start most businesses, it takes a lot of money—working capital. There are two main reasons for most business failures. They are poor management and not enough capital to see the business through to the point of success. Chuck hopes to own his own business one day. He knows he is making money for his employer now. That's fine for the present. He hopes one day to be making that money for himself. But Chuck knows that starting a business is risky. He knows that a business owner faces tremendous challenges and risks. That's why the rewards can be great for the successful person. Chuck is going to be patient, learn all he can, and prepare himself. One day, just maybe, he will take the big plunge.

Another Way of Earning Money—Return on Savings

Besides working for your money, you can have your money work for you! Here's how that works. First, you save some of your money instead of spending it all. Second, you put those savings to work for you. Usually this would be in the form of a savings account which earns interest or you could be one of the young adults who invests in the stock market and enjoys dividends and capital gains. We explain what these terms mean next.

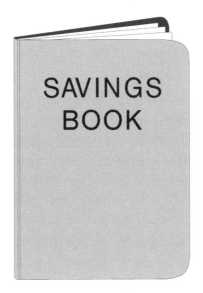

Chuck saves part of his income

Interest

When you put some of your money in a savings account at a financial institution, such as a commercial bank, savings and loan association, or credit union, you are paid interest. You, in effect, are lending money to that institution. The bank will pay you to use your money. Typically, small passbook savings accounts earn at least 3 percent interest per year. On a savings account that had an even $100 in it the whole year, you would earn a little more than $3.

Why a little more? Because of something called compounding. That's where the interest owed you is calculated each day or each month. That interest is added to your account, and your interest for the next period is calculated on the new and higher amount in your account. In effect, you earn interest on your interest.

Interest may not sound like much on $100, but on larger sums it really adds up. If you have a larger amount in savings, often the interest rate can be higher.

This is a good place to describe a "Certificate of Deposit." That's where you have a large sum, usually $1,000 or more, that you agree to leave on deposit for a stated period of time. The institution will pay you a much higher rate of interest. This is because it is a larger amount, and you leave it there for a known period of time.

Dividends and Capital Gains

Many people invest in the stock market. In this case, a person buys shares in the ownership of a company. That person actually becomes one of the owners of the company. While there can be a large potential gain if the company does well, there is also increased risk. If the company makes money, it may pay out part of its profits to shareholders in the form of "dividends." If the company really does well, the stock will increase in value because more people want to buy it. This increase in value represents "capital gains" to the investor. Of course, the stock can lose value. It can make you a nervous wreck as you watch the value move up and down!

Usually, people should only invest in stocks after they have a good chunk of regular savings in a safe place. This way they can afford to take more risk with a part of their savings.

Borrowing Money

From time-to-time we may need to buy something before we have saved enough cash. Maybe we have some savings but don't want to touch them. There can be many situations, such as a medical emergency or major car repairs, which cause us to borrow. Also, we may wish to use something while we pay for it. We figure that the present use of the item, such as an auto like Chuck's, is worth making payments and paying interest. Often, a smart investor will borrow money to invest. Borrowing for legitimate purposes is fine, so long as borrowing is not abused.

How much a person can borrow is determined by several things. Often the most important of these are called "The Three Cs"—Character, Capacity, and Capital. (In lending, "capital" may include "collateral," or something of value that one mortgages as security for a loan.) Character may be the most important. This is a person's reputation. An example would be how promptly the person paid his or her bills in the past. The record of payment is recorded on a "credit report." Later in this book we devote an entire chapter to explaining the role of credit bureaus that produce credit reports on individuals and on business firms. Capacity is a person's ability to repay credit, as determined by his or her "disposable income." Disposable income is income which is not needed for living expenses or already committed for other debt. The last of the three Cs, capital, is often worth the least. Many reputable companies will not extend credit based just on collateral. Character and capacity must also be present. Often one's capital, used as collateral, is required in addition to the first two important qualities.

Collateral is something of value, such as a car, a home, or savings, that is pledged as security on a loan. When you borrow money to buy a car or boat or anything else of significant value, that property, which now belongs to you, becomes collateral. This means that the creditor has a "lien" on the item. If you don't pay as agreed, the lender can take the collateral away from you.

But the collateral may not always pay off the whole remaining debt. In the case of a car loan, if the car is "ragged" out and not worth as much as you owe on it, the creditor may sue you for the difference—called a "deficiency." In that case, you could lose the car and *still owe money!*

A lot of good folks get into serious trouble because they don't understand this. A person must realize that the bank or credit union or finance company, or whoever extended the credit, isn't in the business for the collateral. They are in the money business. That's what they loaned out, and that's what they want back—plus interest.

The better your credit record (character), the higher your income (capacity), and the better your collateral (capital), the more credit for which you can qualify. Unless you have an excellent long-time credit record and have fantastic earnings, you better forget about the Porsche and go for the Chevy.

A down payment can be important when you are borrowing money to buy a big-ticket item, such as a car. The lender wants to know that you are using some of your own money. Now, you may see and hear a lot of ads claiming no money is needed for a down payment. On the bottom of the TV screen, however, a quick and small message flashes—"with approved credit." What that means is your credit better be very good!

Chuck borrowed part of the purchase price of his car. He didn't have a whole lot of credit because of his age. But he had saved a good down payment, and he had a stable earnings record. In another part of this book, we talk about some more important facts of using credit and borrowing money.

Managing Money

Once you get money by earning it, you have to use it wisely. "A fool and his money are soon parted." That's an old saying. It's still true today, and it will be as long as there are fools with money. In a later chapter, we tell you how to develop a savings program. We also explain how to establish relationships with creditors and how to use money services. You also need to know how to protect yourself with insurance. Insurance is so important in life that we devote an entire chapter in this book to it.

One of the guys Chuck works with has a very high-paying job. But he doesn't have much to show for it. He doesn't pay any attention to his business. In spite of making good money, he is constantly going from one money problem to another. In fact, on occasion, he tries to borrow enough money from Chuck to get by till the next payday. And Chuck is only working part-time while he is in school!

There are two facts that counselors at Consumer Credit Counseling Services can tell you. One, there are a lot of people out there with a good standard of living who have never made a lot of money. Two, there are a lot of people who always are in trouble because they can't manage a high income.

Managing money is often called budgeting. Both terms simply mean planning in advance what you will do with your money before you do it. You can't budget what you have already spent. You've already lost the choices. So if you are going to budget, or plan, you must do it in advance.

Some people make a serious mistake in budgeting. They try to account for every penny, or plan things out down to the last cent. That's unnecessary, and it becomes discouraging when they find it is a lot of work. You must leave a little leeway, because no plan can be perfect.

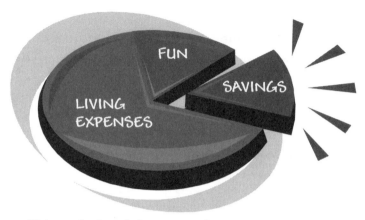

Using a budget helps you make your money last

A basic budget can be quickly and easily made. The first step is to make a budget for a consistent period, such as a month. Next, divide the month into paydays (unless you get one paycheck a month). Then develop a simple budget for each payday within the month. If you have *monthly* bills, you must assign them to a certain payday within the month. For each payday, start by setting aside the correct amount to pay things you are obligated to pay, such as a debt, and for essentials, such as food, shelter, and transportation expense. Whatever is left is *discretionary*, or *disposable, income*. Let's hope there is something left! You should set aside some part of discretionary income for savings.

If you develop a savings habit when you are young, it will stick with you for the rest of your life. You will reap the rewards of that habit later. It is very unusual for someone with a good savings habit to get into financial trouble. The amount, or percent, of your income that you set aside for savings can be flexible, but most experts recommend at least six to eight percent of your income. After determining your savings goal, you can make decisions about how you want to spend the remainder of your income.

A budget should be a living, flexible tool. Life seldom stays the same for long. Therefore, you must be ready to modify your budget as your circumstances change.

People often ask credit counselors how much of their income they should spend for specific purposes. But there is no simple answer. No two people are alike. Different people have different values, different priorities. Thank goodness—otherwise we would all dress exactly alike and eat the same foods! In budgeting, you must decide what is most important for you. Just remember, you can't make each of your "wants" a top priority. Something has to give.

If clothes are the most important thing in your life, that's fine. Just be willing to drive a cheaper car. If a fancy apartment, or home, is sacred to you, that's all right too. But if you want it all, then you better set your career sights high and make yourself of great value. Otherwise you're in for a real crash.

THINGS TO REMEMBER

Money is earned by working for someone else, by owning your own business, or from receiving returns on investments.

Having a good work ethic is essential to keeping a job.

In order to borrow money, one must have *character*, *capacity*, and *capital*.

Starting your own business requires knowledge and capital.

The most common reasons for the failure of a new business are a lack of capital and poor management.

To be secure in a job, you should strive to be worth more than you are actually paid.

A high income does not guarantee a good lifestyle. Income must be managed wisely.

Simple budgeting will help assure financial success.

Chapter Seven

What Is Credit?

Right now, Chuck Taylor is a senior in college. He has worked part-time since he was in high school. You already know a lot about him and that he bought his new car. Yes, he used credit. But he used it wisely.

In this chapter, you learn what credit is, how to get it, and—what's most important—how to use it correctly.

Just about every time you turn on the TV or pick up a newspaper, some merchant is advertising how easy it is to use your credit. Advertising makes it sound good, doesn't it? Credit is good if it is used wisely. In fact, credit is just about the most powerful tool available to the average consumer. It can help you manage your income and have a good standard of living. But credit is just like any other powerful tool. It can hurt you if you don't use it safely.

Let's stop here and define a few terms. *Credit* is created when someone gives you money or something else of value in exchange for your promise to pay at some time in the future. Probably every young person's experience with credit starts with borrowing from Mom or Dad against next week's allowance. Perhaps a friend may ask you to lend him five dollars in exchange for his IOU. Often these informal extensions of credit are simply oral agreements. Nothing is written down on paper. But when you go to the bank to borrow money, the banker will have you sign a legal loan agreement with specific terms. Credit is created in each of these instances.

The phrase *having good credit* means that a person has demonstrated that he or she has the capacity and character to be trusted to repay as promised. In other words, such a person can show that he or she is able and willing to repay credit as promised. In the U.S. economy, credit is readily available to people who have good credit.

Chuck obviously established good credit. Without good credit, he could not have bought that new car unless he had waited until he saved the entire purchase price. Now he is enjoying the rewards that can come from having and using credit intelligently. He is getting to drive the car while he is paying for it.

A *creditor* is the one who extends credit. It could be a person such as a parent or a business firm such as a department store or a bank. Again, the credit is extended in return for a promise to repay, plus interest, on specific terms. The person who gives the promise to repay is a *debtor*. That term is a little on the negative side, so the term *borrower* usually is used. We use these terms a lot in the next several pages.

It's pretty easy for most people to get credit these days. Just look at some of the advertisements. These advertisers want you to use credit so that they can sell more of their products or services. Extending credit can help all kinds of businesses increase their sales and profits. After all, that's what business is all about—sales and profits. Many other kinds of companies, such as banks, savings and loans, consumer finance companies, and credit unions, are actually in the business of selling the use of money.

Because credit can be so easy to get, some people will bite off more than they can chew. Usually, these are people who never learned to budget and are likely to buy something suddenly without giving much thought to the purchase. They really can get themselves into trouble. We said that credit is a powerful tool and must be used with respect. People who abuse credit quickly find themselves with a lot of debt and sometimes little to show for it. Later, when they really need credit badly, they can't get it.

Credit usually is extended by creditors on simple faith and trust. This places the burden of responsibility on a borrower not to abuse that privilege. People who abuse credit hurt not only themselves, but other people as well. A person who does not repay as promised costs everyone else extra in the form of both higher prices of goods and higher interest rates. That's because creditors pass any losses they suffer from bad loans on to the rest of us.

The Advantages of Having and Using Good Credit

The principal advantage of good credit is that it enables you to get what you want or need without having to wait while saving the entire price. Not having to wait can be very important when, for example, an emergency arises. In times of emergency, a person without good credit can be in a real jam. Sometimes the best thing about having good credit is just knowing that it is there if and when needed. You can feel more secure and you can sleep better at night when you have good credit.

Good credit is an advantage when disaster strikes

Of course, a person can survive without using credit. In fact, some people have no choice. They have to get by without credit because no one will grant it to them because they are considered a poor risk. That is, they can't show that they have the ability and willingness to repay loans. All other things being equal, if you manage your income intelligently using credit, you will accomplish much more than a person who has to manage the same income *without* using any form of credit.

A good credit rating also could mean the difference between whether or not you get a particular job you may apply for one day. Employers often get a credit report on job applicants. Why? They want someone who is financially stable and uses good judgment.

Again, one of the most important reasons for having good credit is just plain having it. There is the fantastic feeling of pride and sense of accomplishment in having a good reputation and the security that goes with it. This is a sense of well being that few other things can duplicate. It means that, whether or not you make a lot of money, you keep your word. People know that, and they respect and trust you. And they would be willing to lend money to you.

How to Start Establishing Your Good Credit

The best time to start your good credit is *before* you need it. Like a lot of other good things in life, that takes preparation—thinking ahead.

Here are a few of the things a creditor looks for in all credit applications. He or she looks even more closely at these things in the case of a young person just starting out.

- *Income.* How much do you earn, and how stable is that income? How long have you been employed? Do you earn enough to support the credit you want?

- *Assets.* Do you own anything of value?

- *Savings.* Have you demonstrated a savings habit by gradually building up some savings?

- *Purpose of the credit.* In the case of a direct loan, do you have a sensible and prudent use for the credit?

- *Down payment or collateral.* Can and will you make a partial payment using your own money? Can and will you pledge any asset to back up your promise to pay? Let's say you want to buy a used car costing $2,500, and you have saved a $500 down payment. That's a lot more attractive deal to a creditor than the person who wants a new Corvette and has "zip" for a down payment.

If you fall a little short of some of these items (and most young people do), the creditor may tell you that you need a co-signer. A co-signer is another person who promises to pay the creditor if you don't. This business of co-signing is so important that a whole section on that topic follows later.

Start developing your good reputation before you have to use it. A record of good, responsible behavior will pave the way to getting credit later.

Here are some suggestions that you can use to build good credit quickly:

1. Start a savings habit. If you have savings (and if you're over 18 in most states), you may be able to borrow using your savings as collateral.

2. Never bounce checks. The way you handle your checking account becomes part of your credit record.

3. Never apply for credit just to see if you can get it.

4. Be sensible in what credit you ask for, and pay exactly as agreed. As you start to get a little credit, be patient and don't try for too much too soon.

In time, you will have built a strong record. Then keep it that way! Next time you borrow five bucks from Mom or Dad or a friend, remember your credit is at stake.

Chuck used those tips to start his credit. By the time he was 18, he had savings from his part-time job. He made a loan against those savings, paid it back quickly, and that started his credit. The loan officer remembered him later and was impressed with him.

Evidence of Chuck's financial
responsibility impressed the loan officer

In recent years, there has been a trend to make credit more available to young people. As but one example, credit card companies often send pre-approved credit applications to college students. Lenders have learned that college students, for the most part, will be responsible credit users. Most college students have not yet established favorable credit ratings. But the credit card issuers take some risk, believing that many of these students will become good customers for life.

Another recent trend is the development of "secured" credit cards. This is where a credit card company will provide a credit card to someone who has not established good credit, or maybe even has some blemishes on his or her credit record. But this line of credit must be secured by a saving account! So, you must put up your own savings as security, and you cannot use your savings while the credit line is active. These credit lines usually do not have the most favorable rates and terms.

All About Co-signing

Not every young person is as fortunate as Chuck. In fact, many don't have some of the good things going for them that Chuck does. Even if you are a bit short on some of the factors that a creditor looks at, you may still be able to start your credit with the help of a co-signer. One day, someone may even ask you to co-sign for him or her. You need to learn now what this business of co-signing is all about.

The terms co-signer, co-maker, endorser, and guarantor all mean about the same thing. You and the co-signer both sign a note, which is a promise to pay on specific terms. Then both you and the co-signer are jointly and individually responsible to the creditor for the terms of the note. This means that, if you don't pay for whatever reason, the creditor is going to go after the co-signer. There are no excuses, ifs, ands, or buts. It's that simple.

Co-signing is an excellent means of helping someone start building good credit. But we are here to tell you that it is serious business. You can get Mom, Dad, or whoever co-signed with you all messed up if you are not responsible and mature enough to know what you are doing. Sometimes problems over a co-signed debt cause serious trouble between friends or family members. At worst, these problems can result in financial disaster.

Before you ask someone to co-sign for you, you first should look in the mirror. Would you co-sign for yourself? Do you have your feet on the ground? Is your income stable enough for you to be sure that you can pay back the debt? If it's a bad deal, asking someone to co-sign is a "bummer."

Next, you better hope Mom, Dad, or other co-signer has good credit. If not, their endorsement would be rejected. You see, if they don't have a good record of paying their own debts, why should a creditor believe they will pay your debt if need be?

But there is another problem here. (We are telling you something a lot of moms and dads may not know.) When someone co-signs for someone else, he or she is using some of his or her own credit capacity. In other words, co-signers are expected to be fully able to pay their own bills and have room left over to pay yours, too, if it should become necessary. If Mom and Dad have their hands full financially trying to keep you fed and in designer clothes, they might not be able to co-sign for that car you want. All people, no matter how high their income, have limits on how much they can borrow. There's no exact formula, but there is a limit. That's something you learn more about next.

How Much Can You Borrow?

As we mentioned earlier, how much credit a person can handle depends on several things. Remember the three Cs— Character, Capacity, and Capital. Usually, the more you have of these three things, the more you can borrow. Although character, capacity, and capital cannot be measured exactly, every lender or creditor will judge you on these things. Also, life has a way of throwing curve balls at you causing sudden changes in these factors. For example, your income may drop. Your expenses may increase. Things you own (which can be used as collateral) may increase or decrease in value. The trick in using credit wisely and staying out of trouble is simply not to overdo it.

Earlier we discussed budgeting. This involves sitting down and putting a paper and pencil to work. A budget is made up of three factors: income, expenses, and obligations. Your expenses and obligations must never exceed your income, *with a safety factor built in*. Otherwise, you are in trouble.

Income is the money that you can count on coming in from all sources. Expenses are expenditures on things like food, housing, utilities, gas, and all sorts of other things for which you must have money. Obligations are those things for which you are already committed, such as other debts owed to a bank or department store. If your expected income is far more than the amount you expect to spend plus payments on your obligations, you may have some borrowing capacity.

Sometimes borrowing capacity also depends on other things. If your job is viewed as extremely stable, your credit capacity may be larger than that of someone with the same income but from a job that may not be so certain. The creditor wants to know that you will continue receiving that income.

Often a person with stable income, excellent credit, and assets that have been accumulated over a period of time will have a large borrowing capacity. Often he or she can borrow relatively large sums without even putting up collateral. Wise is the person who has accomplished this. Such a person often has access to borrowing at lower interest rates and on better terms. This is fair, because he or she can demonstrate to the creditor that not much risk would be involved in giving him or her a loan.

To sum all of this up, you are responsible for knowing how much debt you can handle. A little simple budgeting and a balance sheet are tools that you can use to make sure that you don't bite off more than can be chewed. The time to check your credit capacity is before you get into credit trouble!

Use credit carefully to avoid a sea of debt

The Balance Sheet

Along with a budget, a "balance sheet" or a "net worth statement" is useful in determining how much you can borrow.

A balance sheet is really a snapshot of your financial condition as of a specific date. It has three parts. We've reproduced an example of a balance sheet for you. A balance sheet is often called a "Net Worth Statement."

Example of a Simple Balance Sheet

Assets (Things You Own)	Liabilities (What You Owe)
Automobile $3,500	Auto Loan $2,300
Sound System 300	Mom & Dad 900
	Credit Card 100
Jewelry 500	Charge Account 800
Savings 1,000	Total Liabilities $4,100
Check Account................ 300	
Furniture 1,500	Net Worth 3,000
	Total Liabilities
Total Assets $7,100	And Net Worth $7,100

On the left side of the page is the section called *Assets*. Assets are what you own, even if you owe money on them. On the right side of the statement there are two parts. The first is called *Liabilities*. Liabilities are what you owe on debts and other obligations. The second part on the right side is your *Net Worth*, or *Equity*. That's the difference between the value of what you *own* in the assets section and the amount of money you *owe* in the liabilities section. In other words, your liabilities plus your net worth on the right must equal your total assets on the other side. That's why it's called a "Balance Sheet." Both sides have to equal, or be in "balance."

You need not worry too much about making up balance sheets at this point in your life. But, you will have to if you ever apply for some serious credit later. You will want to see your net worth increase each year as you make sure that the value of your assets increases faster than the amount of your liabilities.

We recommend that you stop every so often and make an accounting of your financial accomplishments. Once a year is good enough for most folks. This financial accounting, in essence, will be a balance sheet.

How to Make Your Own Balance Sheet

First, list everything of any significant value that you own. Doing this exercise helps you to remember things that you might otherwise forget. Don't forget that money in your checking or savings account is an asset. If anyone owes you money, then that is an asset too, as long as you know that person will pay you back.

Next, assign your best knowledge of the fair market value to each thing on your list. Fair market value is what something is really worth today, not what you paid for it. A rule of thumb: things like appliances and furniture are now worth about half of what you paid for them as long as the items are in excellent condition. (For a business, assets are listed at their actual historical cost less depreciation, not some estimate of current value.)

Then list the current balance of every debt you owe. Do not overlook any kind of debt you have.

Now you can organize the items into a balance sheet. List assets on the left and liabilities on the right. Add each column. We hope the total of your *Assets* will exceed the total of your *Liabilities*. If so, the difference between the two items will be a positive *Net Worth*. This tells you that you are beginning to accumulate wealth. If your liabilities exceed your assets, then you have a negative net worth. That can imply that your past income has not been spent wisely or that you have too many debts. In either case, your financial condition needs some attention—fast.

All That Glitters

As good as credit is, it's not gold. It's a powerful tool and can bite the hand that doesn't treat it with respect. Handled with care, credit can improve your lifestyle and your sense of self-respect. It can help you in an emergency. However, it is not to be abused.

In the first place, remember that good credit does not increase your income. It doesn't magically make you able to afford things that you cannot pay for through your ability to produce an income. While credit can make buying things much easier, it still won't enable you to keep up with the Joneses if they make a lot more money than you do!

In addition, sometimes the availability of credit can increase temptation too much. If you are too impulsive and can't say no to yourself, good credit can be your worst enemy. Of course, it wouldn't be for long. If you mess things up too badly, you won't have that good credit very long!

*Take care of your credit—stop
and think before you spend*

Credit can be addictive. Weak or impulsive people can get hooked on credit to the point of financial self-destruction. It's just like getting hooked on drugs or alcohol. The ones who think they are too tough or too smart usually are the ones who stupidly find themselves in trouble.

Credit cannot replace the need for savings. There is a time to use credit and a time to pay cash. Don't use credit too frequently or for things for which credit was never intended. It can make you forget that savings are a critical part of your financial life. Then one day you find you have become too dependent on credit. You are caught in a vicious cycle that isn't easily broken.

Some people use a credit card for everyday, routine purchases, but they pay the balance in full each month. That's using credit for convenience. That is fine as long as the individual is a good manager and limits total monthly charges to an amount he or she can pay.

Used intelligently, the advantages of credit almost always outweigh the interest cost. But if you abuse credit and use it poorly, you could find the interest cost consuming a lot of the income you earn. Then you are in a bad situation.

Believe it or not, some people simply should never use credit. They just can't "hack it." It's just like pouring gas on a fire. They will repeatedly get themselves into trouble. These really are not bad people; their skills just lie elsewhere!

Most people will agree that the intelligent use of credit carries more reward than price. But, remember that when you use credit, you are spending your future income—all the more reason to learn how to make wise decisions.

Use credit wisely to gain benefits. Beware of credit abuse. Sometimes you just have to say "no" to yourself and to too much borrowing.

What If Trouble Strikes?
There is risk in everything. Nobody really knows what the future holds. We control most of what happens to us by using good judgment and common sense. However, there are so many uncertainties in life that it can boggle your mind. Will you have a date for the party Saturday night?

Will you fall in love? Will you graduate from college? Will you get a good job? All of these uncertainties and more face each of us every day. We wish we could tell you that uncertainty would one day vanish from your life. But we cannot do that.

What does this have to do with money and credit? A lot! Very few people are going to get out of this life without facing one or more financial crisis. In this section, we tell you some of the things you can do when trouble strikes.

Unexpected illness, loss of a job through no fault of your own, or any other of a number of things can cause financial problems. When adverse circumstances strike, it won't do any good to feel sorry for yourself. You simply have to look for the positive things you can do. You have to make things better.

The first step in dealing with financial trouble is to recognize it quickly. Accept that it's really facing you and that you must do something. You will always have choices, and the worst choice is to stick your head in the sand and ignore the problem. That won't work. The problem will not go away by itself.

Once you accept your problem, you must look around for the choices that are open. You always have choices that can make things better, even if some are painful. List your options, using common sense to think each one through.

If the problem is a loss of income, you must do everything possible to replace that income as quickly as you can. Waiting for a good job to come find *you* just won't cut it. But that's what some people do! You usually should take the first honest job you can get that produces income. It is often easier to get a better job when you are working than it is to find work when you're unemployed.

If the problem is that you've just used too much credit, you must stop using credit until some of the debt is paid off. This is where a lot of people go wrong. They don't want to face how much they owe. So they keep on using credit, waiting for a raise or a promotion to bail them out. And they sink deeper into debt.

If bills come due and you can't pay them right then, sit down and take stock. Make a plan to get back on track. Call each creditor that you owe and explain your problem. If you can show creditors that you have a plan to deal with your situation, they usually are more than happy to help. If you don't call them first, they're going to call you. Then they aren't going to be as pleasant to deal with!

If the problems are too serious for you to handle alone, call a professional. There are non-profit credit counseling companies nearly everywhere. They have experts to help people deal with credit problems. These services are supported primarily by creditors concerned with helping a sincere customer who is in trouble. The CCCS headquartered in Baton Rouge, Louisiana, also has offices in Alexandria, Bossier City, Gonzales, Hammond, Lafayette, Lake Charles, Leesville, Monroe, Natchitoches, New Iberia, Opelousas, Ruston, Shreveport, Zachary and in El Dorado, Arkansas. Our phone number in Baton Rouge is (225) 923-2227. We may be reached from anywhere toll-free at (800) 364-5595. Counseling is available in-person or by telephone.

In choosing a counseling service, ask if they are a member of the National Foundation for Credit Counseling. NFCC members subscribe to standards and practices designed to ensure quality service and financial integrity. Watch out for unscrupulous, so-called "counseling" businesses that can really mess up a person. You should always check with your Better Business Bureau or with one or more of your creditors before seeking help from a questionable source.

In Appendix C and Appendix D, respectively, you will find more complete information on Consumer Credit Counseling Services and Better Business Bureaus.

CCCS agencies can help with debt problems

THINGS TO REMEMBER

Credit is created when someone gives you something of value in exchange for your promise to pay at some time in the future.

The time to establish good credit is before you actually need it.

The main advantage of credit is that you can get what you want or need without first having to save the entire purchase price.

Another great advantage of credit is simply the convenience of being able to use it.

A co-signer can help you to start building good credit.

Co-signing a loan is serious business.

Good credit depends on a person's willingness and ability to fulfill his or her promise to pay as agreed.

You should review your financial condition on a regular basis.

Wise use of credit can help you raise your standard of living. Misuse can lead to serious financial problems.

When people get into serious financial trouble, there are non-profit services that can help them.

Chapter Eight

Where To Borrow Money

The last chapter covered credit—how to use it and how to avoid abusing it. In this and the following chapter, you learn how to borrow, where to seek loans, and how to apply for credit.

Chuck Taylor could have waited to buy his car until he had saved up the entire price. But he had good credit and enough income to be able to borrow some of the money he needed. By saving enough money for his down payment, he had proved both that he had good self-discipline and that he had adequate disposable income to handle credit payments. Because Chuck had a legitimate need for an automobile, had saved a down payment, and had the income with which to safely make the monthly payments, his financing the purchase of an automobile was a good example of the wise use of credit.

When Chuck was ready to borrow money, he had to figure out where to go for a loan. There are many willing lenders eager to do business with responsible customers. Choosing one seemed to be a bit complicated, and Chuck wanted to make a good choice; so, he took the time to learn about the different types of financial institutions.

Financial Institutions

Much of the borrowing, use of credit cards, and most of the saving that you do will involve financial institutions. Unless you plan on never having a job, never making a dime, and never owning anything, you, like Chuck, better know something about financial institutions. All through life you'll be doing business with people who *do* know about those things. You don't want to end up with the short end of the stick.

There are three basic types of financial institutions with which most people do business during their life. We mention each briefly below; then we describe in more detail what they can do for you.

Many services are provided by financial institutions

Depository institutions. These are institutions in which you can deposit your money in a savings or checking account and withdraw it pretty much as you wish. These are usually "full-service" institutions, which also can make loans and issue credit cards. They can take care of most financial needs that people have. Examples are commercial banks, credit unions, and savings and loan associations.

Contractual institutions. Insurance companies and pension funds fall into this category. You make payments to these institutions over a long period of time. You can get your money out only when a particular event occurs. That event could be your death or your retirement.

Entrepreneurial institutions. These companies don't take deposits from customers to get their money. Rather, they borrow the money elsewhere and then lend it to you. The best example of this type is a consumer finance company.

Depository Institutions

There are four major types of depository institutions in the United States—commercial banks, savings and loans associations, credit unions, and money market funds. These are very important to most everyone because they serve us in so many ways.

Commercial Banks

The most important type of depository institution is a commercial bank. More people do business with commercial banks than with any other type of institution. You can find just about any financial product you want. There are about 8,500 commercial banks in the country, and they operate over 55,000 branch locations. The total assets of all banks combined is over $5.5 trillion. Many banks now offer their products on the Internet. In fact, a few don't even have regular offices; they operate only on the Internet.

A lot of folks don't know it, but commercial banks are owned by people just like you. Banks issue shares of stock to the owners in exchange for the investment that the owners originally made. Later, those shares of stock may be sold by one investor to another. Bank stock has value and pays dividends according to the profits the bank makes. Therefore, banks are very much like other businesses, such as Microsoft, General Electric, or Ford Motor Company. They exist to make money for their owners. Banks attempt to offer products that you need and are willing to pay for. They must generate income that exceeds expenses. That's the only way to make a profit.

Banks are very important to us. They accept deposits from the general public. Because of this, they are heavily regulated and supervised by the government. The objective of bank regulation is to make sure that banks are operated in a safe and sound manner so that the money you may have on deposit will be safe. Also, there are regulations to ensure that products are offered with no discrimination on the basis of age, sex, race, religion, or creed.

Your deposit in a commercial bank in the United States is insured up to $100,000 by an agency of the federal government. That agency is the Federal Deposit Insurance Corporation. Commercial banks pay a fee to the FDIC to cover the cost of that insurance. Then, if a bank gets into financial trouble and becomes unable to pay its depositors, the FDIC will arrange for some other bank to take over the deposits or the FDIC will close the bank and pay off the depositors up to the insured amount

Because the FDIC insures deposits, Congress assumes the right to regulate banks. In fact, banks are perhaps the most heavily regulated business firms in the nation. The cost of that regulation, of course, is passed on to consumers in the form of higher prices.

Among the many products a bank offers are checking accounts, savings accounts of all kinds, financing for cars and other things, credit cards, installment loans, cashier's checks, home mortgages, business loans, trust services, safety deposit boxes, 24-hour ATMs (Automated Teller Machines), and many more.

You need to establish a good banking relationship as soon as you can. In fact, it's not too early to do that now! Even if you are too young to use many of the products a bank offers, you can open a savings account at any age. Later, when you need more of the services offered by a bank, at least you will have already established a banking relationship. When you shop for a helpful bank, check out the prices it charges for the products and services you need. Prices tend to vary from one bank to the next.

Credit Unions

These rapidly growing institutions are "cooperatives." That means they exist for the mutual benefit of their members, who are also owners of the credit union. Members may make deposits just like at a bank. They may also receive loans from their credit union provided they have good credit. While the typical credit union is very small, there are many large ones. There are more than 11,000 credit unions across the country. These credit unions serve over 75 million members across the United States. Altogether, credit union members have approximately $360 billion in savings with credit unions. Under federal law, credit unions do not pay income tax on their profits like banks and other institutions do.

Credit unions have to make a profit just like any other business. If a credit union's income for a period of time is not greater than its expenses, the credit union cannot build up its capital. Credit unions need capital to protect the deposits of their members from loss that could arise in the course of making loans to members who do not repay.

Most of the larger credit unions offer many products similar to those offered by banks and savings and loan associations. They finance cars and make personal loans; some even make loans for homes and issue credit cards. Almost all offer what are called "share-draft accounts," which are just like checking accounts at banks.

All credit union savings are insured under federal or private programs. All federal credit unions are insured by the National Credit Union Share Insurance Fund. So, if an insured credit union gets into financial trouble, savers will be protected by that insurance. Like banks, credit unions pay a premium for that insurance. Also like banks, credit unions are closely regulated.

Most credit unions have somewhat restricted membership. Originally, credit unions were established for very small groups, such as employees of a particular company. In recent years, however, memberships have been extended to a much broader base of people. Most credit unions today will allow a relative of a member to be a member!

To join a credit union, all you usually have to do is make a small deposit. Then you are a full member. That entitles you to buy all the products the credit union offers. Remember, though, to qualify for a loan, you must still be able to demonstrate the "three Cs." In many credit unions, regular payroll deductions are arranged for any amount you wish to save. If you have a large enough balance in your account, you may use it as collateral for a loan, often resulting in a lower interest rate for you. Payments on loans made through credit unions are often made through payroll deductions. That is, the monthly payment is taken out of the member's paycheck before the borrower gets the check.

Payroll deduction can be deceptive for some people. A debt owed to a credit union where you work is still a debt. It is the same as if it were owed to a bank or any other creditor. Some people who tend to twist their thinking to suit their own desires may tell themselves, "Well, that's taken out of my check, so I don't have to worry about it." That can be dangerous thinking. You only have so much credit capacity. It doesn't matter to whom you owe the money, it's a debt. And it must be repaid.

Savings and Loan Associations and Other Thrift Institutions

These companies began many years ago as special purpose institutions. Their business originally involved only one goal—providing credit to enable people to buy homes. Of course, to get the money to lend for home mortgages, S&Ls also accepted deposits from savers. Savings and loans grew very rapidly from the early 1950s until the mid-1980s.

In the 1980s, some government regulations, which limited what these institutions could do, were removed. Some

S&Ls branched out into things new to them and to their managements. A large number of S&Ls got into trouble and failed. Many others got caught in a squeeze because their money was loaned out on long-term, low-interest home mortgages at a time when the rates they had to pay savers to attract deposits rose. Since the mid-1980s, the number of S&Ls has decreased sharply to about 1,600. That number includes other types of thrift institutions, as well. Total assets of the insured thrift institutions total about $1.1 trillion.

S&Ls, like banks, are insured by the full faith and credit of the federal government. All depositors are protected up to the $100,000 limit. So, if your savings are less than that amount and in an S&L, your money is as safe as if it were in a bank.

Today, most S&Ls and other types of thrift institutions offer many of the products that banks do.

Money Market Mutual Funds

If this book had been written before 1980, there would be nothing in it about money market mutual funds. That's because, for all practical purposes, they didn't exist! Today, however, many people hold some of their money in these funds. Those funds are offered to savers by investment banking firms such as Merrill Lynch. MMMFs are depository types of institutions, and you can actually write checks against your balance.

Usually the interest rate paid on MMMF deposits exceeds that paid by other institutions, but these funds are not regulated very much. Also, they are not insured by any agency of the federal government. Many are very safe and well managed, but there are so many that you cannot easily get information about all of them. However, they do represent an alternative place for people to deposit some excess money and earn a higher rate. Remember that higher interest usually involves higher risk.

Don't go to a money market mutual fund company and ask for a loan—they will laugh you right out of the place!

Contractual Financial Institutions

Earlier, we defined these institutions as those in which you put money over a period of time. When a particular event occurs, you get your money back, including some interest or other gain. The two major types of these are pension funds and life insurance companies.

In the case of life insurance, each month or each year you make a payment called a premium. The insurance company takes these premiums paid in by all of their policyholders and invests that money. Depending on the terms of the policy, you get an agreed amount of money back at some future age or your beneficiary gets it when you die.

You may not be thinking about retirement now, but one day you really *will* be concerned about it. Probably your ability to retire will be related to a pension fund. A pension fund works like a life insurance company does. You or your employer (or both of you) make payments every month or every year into the pension fund. That money is invested. When you retire, you begin to draw out your pension benefits. Usually, those benefits are paid monthly for as long as you live. But this is not always the case, because there are many different kinds of retirement plans and pension funds. By the way, many large banks have "trust departments" that handle investments for people and pension plans for employers.

This is a good place to mention a benefit that many employers offer. It is called a 401(k) salary deferral plan. The "401(k)" name is simply a reference to the part of the federal tax law that makes this plan legal. In a 401(k) plan, an employee may "defer" before-tax income. Defer means to postpone or delay. In this kind of plan, you are deferring income until some point in the future, and you do not pay income tax in the current year on the amount of income that you defer.

Deferring before-tax income provides the saver an incredible advantage. For you to save money in the regular fashion, you do so with after-tax dollars. In other words, you have to earn, for example, $100 to save $80—the $20 went to pay income tax to the federal government. Then you have only $80 working for you and earning interest. But if you can save before-tax dollars, you would have the entire $100 in your account and the entire $100 earning interest for you. Normally you would also have to pay income tax on interest that you earn. But, in a 401(k) plan, not only are you able to save before-tax dollars, but the earnings, or interest, are allowed to grow untaxed also. You cannot escape taxation forever—eventually the tax man cometh. When you draw this money out, usually around retirement, you must pay taxes on it. But even so, this plan is very much to an employee's advantage for two reasons. One, you end up with more money. Two, the tax bite is lower because, at retirement, most people are in a lower tax bracket.

And, there is a real good kicker. Some employers who sponsor this kind of plan will "match" your deferral. That is, the company also will put some of its money into your 401(k) account as an incentive for you to save under that plan. A match does not necessarily mean dollar for dollar. It may be, for example, a 50 percent match. That means that, for every $10 you save, the employer will put up an additional $5. With a match, you really build up some big bucks in your account!

Another factor that makes these plans attractive is how easily and painlessly they can work. If your employer offers the plan, you simply sign up, and the amount you choose is deducted from your pay each payday. If you sign up for $10 each payday, your take-home pay will be reduced by less than $10. How much less depends on your tax bracket. Tax brackets are explained in Chapter 14. This is how the "before-tax" feature works.

To gain the benefit of these plans, there are costs. The gain is the tax savings and the building of your future security. What you give up is the current use of the money that you put into the plan. You can't tap your 401(k) plan any time you need a little extra money. If you draw money from plans like this before age 59½, you have to pay penalties.

Not all employers offer plans like this. So, to help other people save for retirement, the government allows what is called an "IRA." This stands for Individual Retirement Account. Most everyone, except extremely high-income people, can benefit from an IRA. You can open one with a bank or other qualified institution, and deposit up to $2,000 each year. If you are not eligible for a 401(k) or other employer-sponsored retirement plan, you get to deduct this amount from your taxable income when you file your federal tax return. The concept is very similar to a 401(k), except it takes more discipline. You have to make the payment into your IRA—it does not automatically come out of your paycheck. The earnings from an IRA are tax-deferred, just as in a 401(k).

Investing part of your income into a retirement plan such as a 401(k) or an IRA provides financial growth for your future

We tell you about these things because they are important. And, by getting this far in this book, you have demonstrated the maturity to be able to understand these things and begin to think and plan ahead. That's what financial responsibility is all about. Use of knowledge and information like this is how people accumulate wealth and secure their financial future. Learning about these things, and taking advantage of them like this is what sets some people apart from others.

Entrepreneurial Financial Institutions

These business corporations borrow huge sums of money in the financial markets. In turn, they lend money out in smaller amounts to individuals and sometimes to other businesses. The most common example of this kind of company is a consumer finance or small loan company. These companies do not offer any other service; they just specialize in making relatively small loans to individuals.

Consumer finance companies got started to help fill a need for credit. They continue today as an important source of credit for many people and for many reasons. In some cases, a person may be a good credit risk, but doesn't qualify for a bank loan for one reason or another. In other cases, consumer finance companies may be a little more likely to grant credit to someone who appears to be a greater risk. The small loan company deals with fewer customers and generally knows them better. Also, a small loan company may accept collateral that a bank may not. Many other types of lenders simply will not make small loans involving less than, say, $1,500. So consumer finance companies fill a need in the marketplace.

Most credit granted by a consumer finance company is in the form of "installment" loans. You borrow a specific amount of money, and you pay it back in regular monthly payments for an agreed number of months. This is a good form of credit for people who might tend to overspend with a credit card.

In many cases, the interest rate consumer finance companies charge is higher than that available from some other sources of credit. But we've already pointed out that they provide loans that are not attractive to many other lenders. All in all, consumer finance companies provide a very valuable service and fill an important need for a lot of people.

Captive automobile finance companies are a kind of entrepreneurial institution. They are associated with and owned by the major automobile manufacturing companies. Examples are Ford Motor Credit Corporation, General Motors Acceptance Corporation, and Chrysler Credit Corporation. If you buy a car, the dealer may try to get you to finance the car through one of these lenders. Like anything else, remember to shop around for the best deal on your auto loan.

Chuck Taylor checked out several financial institutions when he was ready to buy his car. In fact, he looked up several lenders on the Internet just like he got prices on cars from several web sites. He ended up borrowing from the place where he had his savings account, which he had started years ago. These people knew him and had treated him well, and he got a relatively low interest rate on his loan.

THINGS TO REMEMBER

The three basic types of financial institutions are depository institutions, contractual institutions, and entrepreneurial institutions.

Banks, credit unions, and savings and loan associations are important depository institutions.

Insurance companies and pension funds are the main types of contractual institutions.

Consumer finance companies are entrepreneurial institutions. They provide a specialized service, often willing to make smaller loans than other institutions.

Lending money is a competitive business, with many institutions offering loan products.

Borrowers can check out several lenders (including some on the Internet).

Chapter Nine

Borrowing From a Financial Institution

Selecting a financial institution was only Chuck's first step in getting a car loan. There was more for him to learn and understand before he got the loan. Some things he had heard about before, but much was new to him. After reading this, you'll be way ahead of where Chuck was back then.

Borrowing money usually is simple for people who have good credit. From earlier chapters you already have learned how to start your credit. However, there are some other important things that you, Chuck, or any borrower needs to understand when you borrow money. Let's look at some of these things.

What's involved in making a loan?

Interest Rates

When financial institutions extend credit to you and others, they expect to be rewarded! That reward is their income and profit. Not only do they expect the money they lend to be repaid, but they must charge interest for the use of the money. The interest they collect is their income. It must cover all expenses plus produce a profit. Among their expenses is the cost to them of the money they lend. Another type of expense is the losses they incur when some people don't pay them back. When someone skips out or takes bankruptcy, lenders pass that cost on to you and to other borrowers in the form of higher interest rates.

The amount of interest you pay to borrow money depends on two things: (1) the interest rate and (2) the period of time you have use of the money. Let's look first at the interest rate.

There is a federal law called the "Truth in Lending Act." Among other things, that law requires all lenders to express the interest rate in terms of "APR," or Annual Percentage Rate. We're not going to bore you with the math of how that rate is calculated. The important thing is that all lenders must calculate the interest rate the same way, so that you can compare rates charged by different lenders.

While it's a good idea to compare interest rates, you may not always want to borrow from the cheapest source. There are other factors that can be very important. For example, you may have a good relationship with a certain institution. That relationship can be very valuable, as Chuck found out. The people at that institution know you, and you know them. Finding a good lender and sticking with him or her can be very important to you. Of course, if the rates are way out of line compared to those offered by other lenders, that's another matter. If possible, however, you should stick with one lender and build a good relationship over a long time. The lender will value your good business and will compete to keep that business.

Remember, the better your credit is, the more valuable your business is to a lender—also, the more likely you are to get a lower interest rate.

There are other factors that affect interest rates in general. Inflation, for example, is one. If we are in a period in which prices are rising, interest rates usually rise also. If a lot of people and businesses are borrowing a lot of money, loan demand is high. That also will tend to cause interest rates to increase. Remember, interest is the price of money and credit. So, the supply and demand factors described in Chapter Three apply to credit as well as other things.

Other Costs of Borrowing

Insurance

There will often be other costs in addition to interest. Most lenders will offer to sell you a "credit life" insurance policy. That way the lender will be repaid by the insurance company in the event of your death. In some states, credit life insurance may be optional. In other states, the lender may require that it be purchased. If you agree to purchase this insurance, the lender will offer to include the premium in the amount you finance.

If you are financing an automobile, you may be required to buy property insurance, such as collision and comprehensive, to protect the collateral. When you obtain a mortgage for a home, the lender will require you to purchase property insurance. When Chuck financed his car, he had to purchase insurance to cover theft or damage to the car in the event he had an accident.

It is important that you learn about the different types of insurance. In the last paragraph, we briefly mentioned collision and comprehensive insurance. Nearly every state requires by law that you purchase liability coverage, but that is a totally different type of insurance. Make sure you study Chapter 12, which covers the basics of insurance.

If the lender requires that insurance be purchased, remember that you are not required to buy the insurance from the lender. You may obtain acceptable coverage from whatever source you wish. So, shop around for the lowest cost. You may find an insurance provider on the Internet.

Penalties

If you do not pay an obligation as agreed, you can count on there being some stiff penalties for late payments. If you get behind on your payments, it will cost you money, and it will affect your credit rating. If you really get into trouble with a debt, you may be sued. Then, you must pay attorney fees and court costs

Other Costs

There may be other costs and fees, but the law requires that these be disclosed to you when you borrow money. When you make a loan, the lender is required by law to provide you a Disclosure Statement. This shows you all costs of the transaction, including the interest rate. Most state laws permit some sort of one-time charge by the lender for setting up the loan. This and any other charges will be revealed on the "Disclosure Statement."

Term, or Maturity of the Loan

Often other terms can be as important as the APR, or interest rate. The faster you pay back the money, all other things being equal, the less is your interest cost. You may be attracted to small monthly payments that result from stretching a loan out over a long period of time; but such an arrangement can be costly. Not only will you end up paying back more dollars, but you will be paying for a longer period of time. Making payments each month gets old. But there is another important factor here, as well. Remember credit capacity? The faster you pay a debt back, the faster you regain that amount of your credit capacity. In practical terms, it can mean that you can use your credit again sooner to buy something else.

Most consumer-type loans are repaid in installments. You pay a set amount each month for a given number of months. This is the most convenient way to repay for most people, but there can be other ways.

In contrast to the installment loan, there is the term loan. With a term loan, you pay back the loan in full all at once at the end of the agreed time. This time can be for any period agreed upon, but most often is 90 days. At the end of that time, the principal (amount borrowed) and the interest must be repaid. Often the lender will agree beforehand that you may pay only the interest due and sign a new note for another 90 days—that is, if you maintain your good credit.

Collateral

As long as your credit is excellent and the amount of credit you want is not excessive, you may get a loan on your "signature." In that case, you need no collateral. But usually a lender requires that you pledge certain assets (something of value that you own) as security or collateral for your loan. So another factor that you will consider in making a loan is the collateral requirement.

When you buy something expensive on credit, that item almost always becomes collateral. When Chuck bought his new car, a mortgage was recorded in favor of the lender. That means that, until the loan is repaid, the car is pledged as security.

There's a minor detail worth mentioning here. When you mortgage something, you cannot sell that property without first paying the debt owed. Until Chuck's car is paid for, he can't sell it without making arrangements with the lender. He might trade the car in before it is fully paid for. If he does, he will have to arrange to add the balance he owes to the amount of the new loan. That may be okay as long as Chuck has built up what is called "equity" in his automobile. For there to be equity, the car must be worth more than the amount still owed on the mortgage.

Many young people finance their first new car for a very long term. This is in an attempt to get their monthly payments low, and perhaps because they may not have yet saved enough money for a large down payment. Then, before they have paid long enough to build up equity, they get tired of that car and want another. They may find out that the value of the car is less than the amount they still owe. This situation is called being "under water" or "upside down" on the loan.

Making the Loan

After you have established good credit and a relationship with a particular bank, S&L, credit union, or finance company, it usually just takes a phone call or a few clicks on your computer keyboard to request a loan. Everything can be arranged in advance. All that would remain is for you to drop by to sign the note and get the money.

If you haven't established a relationship with a lender, you'll need to find an institution. First, check with the bank where you have your checking or savings account. If that doesn't work out, ask your friends where they have borrowed. Perhaps they can refer you to a good creditor. Increasingly, lenders have web sites on the Internet. Check them out. Some even let you apply for a loan online.

Let's hope you've done some of the things we talked about in the section on establishing credit. If you don't have any credit or savings, have only, say, three months on a shaky job, and have no co-signer, forget it. But let's assume some other things. First, you're over 18. That's the age of *majority*, which means at least you are legally capable of obligating yourself. Second, you worked part-time during school and have a little money in savings. Third, now you are working full-time, or you may still be living with family while working part-time and in school. In any case, you have *discretionary income*. That means you make enough money to take on a credit obligation.

When applying for a loan, prepare yourself by thinking through some questions. What do you want to borrow the money for? Would *you* lend money for that purpose? How much do you really need to borrow? What is it that you want to buy? Have you shopped around? Next, spend a few minutes with paper and pencil and work up a budget. Prepare a list of any existing obligations. All of this only takes a few minutes, and you've accomplished two important things. One, you should now know whether or not you have any business asking for a loan, and two, you are ready to make a good impression on the person to whom you apply

When you apply for a loan, the lender will ask you some questions. You need to have answers. Make sure you know how much your gross income is and how much your net income (take-home pay) is. Take-home pay is the amount you earned less payroll deductions for things like retirement, insurance, income taxes, and Social Security taxes. There is more about income and Social Security taxes in Chapter 14.

Next, contact the bank, credit union, S&L, or finance company you've chosen, and tell someone that you would like to come in to discuss a loan. You should take along your paycheck stubs just in case. It wouldn't hurt to take with you a copy of your federal income tax return for last year. When you get there, let's hope you've dressed neatly and have a decent haircut. Remember what we said about eye contact? Simply introduce yourself and go for it!

If you choose to apply on the Internet, you will have a less personal experience. But you still will have to answer the same types of questions on the lender's interactive web site. Increasingly, people are applying for loans on the

Internet. For the lenders, the cost of delivering consumer loan products electronically is falling, while the cost of delivering those products through people in bank buildings is rising. Technology, including credit scoring, makes Internet banking possible.

The Credit Application

As Chuck knew, you can't just walk into a financial institution, get the money, and walk out—at least not if you haven't already established a good credit relationship with that institution. Your first step is the application for credit. The lender has to know who you are, where you live and work, and a lot of other details. While a credit application may seem intimidating, it's really not. Study the illustrations of a credit application. If you were a lender getting ready to make a loan decision, you, too, would want this information.

Look at the information provided by the two applicants. To which one would you be willing to make a loan?

An important rule: Always be accurate and completely truthful in giving information on a credit application. Whether you provide it at the bank or online, never violate this rule. The application requires your signature, and you are stating that the information is accurate. In fact, it is a federal criminal offense to knowingly lie on a credit application to a federally insured financial institution.

After the application is complete, the lender will check your credit rating at one or more credit bureaus. The lender probably will verify your employment and other information you have given. You see, a lender has a great responsibility to control the risk. He or she must make every effort to make good loans. It's not a question of the lender not believing you; the loan officer simply is doing his or her job.

Today, most decisions on consumer credit applications are made by a computer. The process is called credit scoring. All of the information you provide is translated into a number, or score, by a complex computer program. The score you receive determines whether or not you get the loan.

Types of Loans

There are many different kinds of loans available to individuals. Lenders often call these "products." They design and advertise them to make them attractive. Remember that this is a free market economy, and there is competition for your business. There are car loans, signature loans, consolidation loans, and home mortgage loans, just to name a few. Some institutions make nearly every kind of loan there is. Others aggressively specialize in one or two kinds. A few, like the captive auto finance companies, only make one kind of consumer-type loan. When selecting a lender, make sure it offers the kind you need.

Simple Interest Loans

In this kind of loan, the interest owed on the current balance is calculated each month and subtracted from your payment. The amount left is called a "principal" payment. This is what is subtracted from your balance to determine how much you still owe. All normal home financing is done this way, and many institutions use this method for automobile financing.

In simple interest loans, the amount of interest taken out of payments during the early part of the loan will be higher. This is because the balance is the highest (you owe the creditor more). As you make payments over the life of the loan, the interest drops because you owe less each month.

Add-on Loans

In the case of add-on loans, the total amount of interest you will pay for the entire expected term of the loan is

APPLICATION FOR LOAN
MONEYWISE NATIONAL BANK

Equal Housing LENDER

Please Print

You REQUEST AN ADVANCE OF $ 350.00	PURPOSE SOUND SYSTEM

APPLICANT

DRIVER'S LIC. NO. 1068833	STATE LA	

FIRST NAME WILLIAM	INITIAL L.	LAST NAME SLATER	DATE OF BIRTH 9-30-79

SOCIAL SECURITY NO. 480-22-1168	MARITAL STATUS ☒ Single ☐ Married ☐ Separated	NO. OF DEPENDENTS Ø	HOME TELEPHONE NO. 555-6651

ACTUAL PRESENT RESIDENCE 1020 NORTH ST. ☐ Rent ☐ Own   MONTHLY PAYMENT $ 250.00

CITY ANYWHERE	STATE LA	ZIP CODE 70732	COUNTY ALLEN	YEARS 0	MONTHS 5

FORMER STREET ADDRESS 214 TEXAS ST.	CITY ANYWHERE	STATE TEXAS	ZIP CODE 22314	YEARS 12	MONTHS 2

PERMANENT STREET ADDRESS SAME AS ABOVE	CITY	STATE	ZIP CODE	YEARS	MONTHS

ARE YOU A CITIZEN OF THE UNITED STATES? ☒ YES ☐ NO	IF NOT, DO YOU HAVE PERMANENT RESIDENCE STATUS? ☐ YES ☐ NO	PERMANENT RESIDENCY NO.

NAME OF NEAREST RELATIVE NOT LIVING WITH YOU — NAME LOUIS SLATER — STREET ADDRESS 214 TEXAS ST. ANYWHERE TX 22314 — STATE/ZIP — PHONE 713-555-8280 — RELATIONSHIP FATHER

OCCUPATION TIME EMPLOYED

CURRENT EMPLOYER (IF SELF-EMPLOYED, LIST COMPANY INCOME VERIFICATION REQUIRED) JOSEPH JOHNSON	POSITION STOCK CLERK	YEARS 0	MONTHS 8

BUSINESS STREET ADDRESS 8861 GROVE BLVD.	CITY ANYWHERE	STATE LA	ZIP CODE 70832	BUSINESS PHONE 555-9134

PREVIOUS EMPLOYER	ADDRESS	POSITION	YEARS	MONTHS

JOB INCOME (MONTHLY NET) | SOURCES OF ADDITIONAL INCOME (FOR EXAMPLE, STOCKS, REAL ESTATE, RETIREMENT, ETC.) Child support, alimony, or separate maintenance income need not be revealed unless you wish to have it considered as a basis for repaying this obligation.

APPLICANT $ 400.00	SOURCE: PARENT	AMOUNT: $ 200.00
CO-APPLICANT $	SOURCE:	AMOUNT: $
TOTAL $ 400.00	SOURCE:	AMOUNT: $

COMPLETE FOR JOINT APPLICATION

	NAME	DATE OF BIRTH	RELATIONSHIP
SOCIAL SECURITY NO.	DRIVERS LIC. NO.	STATE	EMPLOYER	POSITION	BUSINESS PHONE	YEARS	MONTHS

CREDIT REFERENCES PLEASE LIST ALL YOUR DEBTS. LIST CREDIT UNIONS, BANKS, FINANCE COMPANIES, DEPARTMENT STORE REFERENCES (OPEN)

Creditor Name/Address & Account No./Collateral	Monthly Payment	Balance Owed	Pay-Off Balance
	TOTAL $		

IN THE LAST 10 YEARS HAVE YOU DECLARED BANKRUPTCY OR FILED A PETITION FOR CHAPTER 13?	Y ☐	N ✓	HAVE YOU HAD PROPERTY FORECLOSED UPON OR GIVEN TITLE OR DEED IN LIEU THEREOF IN THE LAST 7 YEARS?	Y ☐	N ☐

PERSONAL FINANCIAL STATEMENT

Assets	Value	Liabilities	pmt/month	balance	date opened
Checking Acct. (Bank) CITIZENS	$ 100.00	House Pmt/Rent	$ 250.00	$	
Savings Acct. (Bank) CITIZENS	$ 300.00	Co.:			
Savings Acct. (Bank)	$	Auto Pmt.	$	$	
Stock/Bonds (itemize)	$	Co.:			
Life Ins. Cash Value	$	Credit Cards	$	$	
	$	Co.:			
Household Goods (estimate)	$	Insurance			
Other Assets BIKE	$ 50.00	Bank Loans	$	$	
			$	$	
Auto: Year — Make	$	Other (alimony, child support, home owners assn., etc.)			
Auto: Year — Make	$		$		
TOTAL ASSETS	# 450.00	**TOTAL LIABILITIES**		# 0	

APPLICANT'S SIGNATURE William L. Slater	SEAL	DATE 3/1/00

APPROVED YES NO

APPLICATION FOR LOAN
MONEYWISE NATIONAL BANK

Equal Housing LENDER

Please Print

You REQUEST AN ADVANCE OF $ **650.00**   PURPOSE **Auto Repairs**

APPLICANT

DRIVER'S LIC. NO. **1032213**	STATE **LA**	

FIRST NAME **Mary**	INITIAL **B.**	LAST NAME **Brown**	DATE OF BIRTH **1-10-77**

SOCIAL SECURITY NO. **101-31-6500**	MARITAL STATUS ☒ Single ☐ Married ☐ Separated	NO. OF DEPENDENTS **-0-**	HOME TELEPHONE NO. **555-5260**

ACTUAL PRESENT RESIDENCE **1015 Pine St., Apt. 1051**	☒ Rent ☐ Own	MONTHLY PAYMENT $ **300.00**

CITY **Anywhere**	STATE **LA**	ZIP CODE **70733**	COUNTY **Allen**	YEARS **2**	MONTHS **3**

FORMER STREET ADDRESS **3644 4th St.**	CITY **Anywhere**	STATE **GA**	ZIP CODE **22341**	YEARS **15**	MONTHS **0**

PERMANENT STREET ADDRESS **1015 Pine St., Apt. 1051**	CITY **Anywhere**	STATE **LA**	ZIP CODE **70733**	YEARS	MONTHS

ARE YOU A CITIZEN OF THE UNITED STATES? ☒ YES ☐ NO   IF NOT, DO YOU HAVE PERMANENT RESIDENCE STATUS? ☐ YES ☐ NO   PERMANENT RESIDENCY NO.

NAME OF NEAREST RELATIVE NOT LIVING WITH YOU: NAME **Susan Jones**   STREET ADDRESS **411 Iron St.**   CITY **Anywhere**   STATE/ZIP **GA 82331**   PHONE **606-555-8280**   RELATIONSHIP **Sister**

OCCUPATION   TIME EMPLOYED

CURRENT EMPLOYER (IF SELF-EMPLOYED, LIST COMPANY INCOME VERIFICATION REQUIRED) **Sam's Wholesale**	POSITION **Secretary**	YEARS **1**	MONTHS **11**

BUSINESS STREET ADDRESS **911 South Blvd.**	CITY **Anywhere**	STATE **LA**	ZIP CODE **70832**	BUSINESS PHONE **555-1163**

PREVIOUS EMPLOYER **ABC Cleaners**	ADDRESS **Anywhere, LA 70832**	POSITION **Cashier**	YEARS **2**	MONTHS **4**

JOB INCOME (MONTHLY NET)   SOURCES OF ADDITIONAL INCOME (FOR EXAMPLE, STOCKS, REAL ESTATE, RETIREMENT, ETC.) Child support, alimony, or separate maintenance income need not be revealed unless you wish to have it considered as a basis for repaying this obligation.

APPLICANT $ **950.00**	SOURCE:	AMOUNT: $
CO-APPLICANT $	SOURCE:	AMOUNT: $
TOTAL $ **950.00**	SOURCE:	AMOUNT: $

COMPLETE FOR JOINT APPLICATION

	NAME	DATE OF BIRTH	RELATIONSHIP

SOCIAL SECURITY NO.	DRIVERS LIC. NO.	STATE	EMPLOYER	POSITION	BUSINESS PHONE	YEARS	MONTHS

CREDIT REFERENCES

PLEASE LIST ALL YOUR DEBTS. LIST CREDIT UNIONS, BANKS, FINANCE COMPANIES, DEPARTMENT STORE REFERENCES (OPEN).

Creditor Name/Address & Account No./Collateral	Monthly Payment	Balance Owed	Pay-Off Balance
Brock's Department Store	75.00	225.00	
World Insurance Co.	84.00 Monthly		
	TOTAL $		

IN THE LAST 10 YEARS HAVE YOU DECLARED BANKRUPTCY OR FILED A PETITION FOR CHAPTER 13?	Y	N ✓	HAVE YOU HAD PROPERTY FORECLOSED UPON OR GIVEN TITLE OR DEED IN LIEU THEREOF IN THE LAST 7 YEARS?	Y	N

PERSONAL FINANCIAL STATEMENT

Assets	Value	Liabilities	pmt/month	balance	date opened
Checking Acct. (Bank) **Moneywise National Bank**	$ **600.00**	House Pmt/Rent	$ **300.00**	$	
Savings Acct. (Bank) **Sam's Credit Union**	$ **1,200.00**	Co.:			
Savings Acct. (Bank)	$	Auto Pmt.	$	$	
Stock/Bonds (itemize)	$	Co.:			
Life Ins. Cash Value	$	Credit Cards	$ **75.00**	$	
	$	Co.:			
Household Goods (estimate)	$ **3,000.00**	Insurance	$ **84.00**	$	
Other Assets	$	Bank Loans	$	$	
	$		$	$	
Auto: Year **1996** Make **Ford**	$ **5,200.00**	Other (alimony, child support, home owners assn., etc.)			
Auto: Year Make	$		$		
TOTAL ASSETS	# **10,000.00**	TOTAL LIABILITIES			

Everything I have stated in this application is correct to the best of my knowledge. MoneyWise National Bank is authorized to check my credit, employment history, obtain a credit report, and to answer questions about their credit experience with me. I understand that it may be a federal crime punishable by fine or imprisonment, or both, to knowingly make any false statements concerning any of the above facts as applicable under the provisions of the United States Criminal Code.

APPLICANT'S SIGNATURE **Mary B. Brown**	SEAL	DATE **3-1-00**

APPROVED   YES   NO

added to the amount you borrow. You sign the note for this total amount. It may seem large because it includes what you borrow plus the interest for the time you use the money. As long as you make payments on time, your entire payment is subtracted from the balance. If you pay off an add-on loan in advance, a "rebate" is calculated and subtracted from the gross balance. Because you incur most of the interest expense in the early part of the term when you owe more, the rebate may seem small.

Short-Term vs. Long-Term Borrowing

The total cost of borrowing depends on a combination of factors. These include interest rate, the term of the loan (maturity), and other costs such as insurance and fees. There is a simple fact that not enough people have learned. The most important way to reduce interest costs when using credit is to repay a debt as quickly as possible. While the interest rate is important, the amount of time you use someone else's money often has a much bigger impact on your cost of using credit.

Look at the examples given on the following pages. The first illustrates how you can pay for a home in 15 years for only slightly larger monthly payments than for a 30-year mortgage. The second shows you how much you can save by financing a car for three years instead of for five. While the monthly payments are larger, the savings are great. You will build equity much faster.

We use an assumed interest rate in these examples. In addition, we use what is called "simple interest" calculations. These examples do not include insurance premiums or other charges in the *amount financed*. You learned in this book that you do not have to purchase credit life insurance from the lender as a requirement for a loan. If the loan is for an automobile, a creditor may require that you keep the collateral insured for the life of the mortgage. You can often save money by arranging for the collision and comprehensive insurance on your own.

Home ownership will probably be important to you one day

Financing a Home

While buying your own home may not be in the cards for you right now, let's start with this example. It involves a "starter" home, maybe not the castle in your dreams.

Sales Price .... $90,000   (money going to the seller)
Closing Costs.................. $750   (costs associated with making the loan)
Points .... $900   (another cost associated with the loan)
Down Payment .... ($9,000)   (10% of the sales price)
Amount Financed..... $82,650   (this is what your mortgage will be)

For a conventional 30-year mortgage at 8.00 percent interest, the monthly payments will be **$606.46**. The same mortgage, but for 15 years, requires monthly payments of **$789.85**.

The monthly payments for half the time are not double! They are only $183.39 more, or 30 percent higher. Now let's look at how much you save by going for the higher payments.

In the case of the 30-year loan, you would make 360 payments (30 years times 12 months). You would pay back a total of $218,325.60 over the term of the loan.

For the 15-year loan, you would make 180 monthly payments (15 times 12). At $789.85 per payment, you would pay back $142,173.00 over the 15-year period.

So, by swallowing the higher payments, you save $76,152.60 ($218,325.60 minus $142,173.00)! Not only that, but your home is paid for in half the time. Moreover, with the shorter loan, you would lower the balance much more quickly and build "equity" faster. You might be able to move up to a nicer home by using that equity.

The example we have given you assumed an 8.00 percent loan. While interest rates will fluctuate over time, in recent years that rate has been fairly typical. In addition, the interest rate on a 15-year loan will always be smaller, other factors being constant. So, the actual saving on the 15-year loan is even greater than our example shows.

Don't let the large payback numbers scare you. If you don't buy a home, you would have to pay rent. So, you would still pay out some big bucks over 15 or 30 years. The interest on a home loan is deductible from your taxable income. This means that you would pay less income tax; so, the monthly payments would be somewhat reduced on an after-tax basis.

Bi-Weekly Payments

There is still another trick in paying back a mortgage on a home and saving even more money. Some lending institutions will allow you to make half-payments every other week. Such an arrangement works well if you have a job that provides a paycheck every other week. This means you make 26 half-payments in a year, or the equivalent of 13 monthly payments. This will not only build equity faster, but will save even more interest costs. Don't arrange this unless the mortgage also allows you to switch to normal monthly payments if you should ever want to. You may change jobs and start getting paid once a month or on the first and fifteenth day of the month rather than every Friday.

One more thing about arranging a mortgage. Even if you agree to the longer mortgage, make sure it allows you to make extra payments on the principal without penalty.

Then you can voluntarily make larger or extra payments to reduce the balance and save interest costs. If you commit to the shorter mortgage, the lender usually will give you a lower interest rate.

ARMs—Adjustable Rate Mortgages

For many decades, nearly all loans to purchase homes were made with an interest rate that stayed the same for the entire life of the mortgage—30 years or otherwise. These loans are called fixed-interest loans because the interest rate didn't change. This is no longer the case. Way back in the 1970s and 1980s, we saw some rather wide swings in interest rates. When interest rates increased, the lenders had to pay more for the money they had loaned out on fixed-rate mortgages. Lenders were caught with millions of dollars in outstanding loans made when rates were low. When rates rose, many lenders quickly found themselves in trouble. They were selling a product below cost—and that won't work very long. So, in the early 1980s, adjustable-rate mortgages became an alternative to the fixed-rate loan. Today, a large proportion of home loans are made on an adjustable-rate basis. Adjustable-rate mortgages are called ARMs.

An ARM is a mortgage that has a variable rate that "floats" with some specified index of market rates, such as prime rate. When that index changes, the interest rate on the ARM, subject to limitations, will also change. So, if the interest on an ARM changes, the payment that the homeowner makes each month also changes.

In a mortgage contract, there may be provisions that limit how much the interest (and therefore the monthly payments) may go up or down. As only an exaggerated example, if interest rates double in one year during the life of an ARM, the rate the homeowner pays could not double.

Is an ARM a good bet for someone wishing to purchase a home? The answer depends. An ARM protects the lender from being hurt if the rate the lender has to pay for money rises. So, in return for this protection, the lender offers inducements to the borrower to choose this type of mortgage. These inducements usually are in the form of a cheaper rate guaranteed for the first year or so of the mortgage. If interest rate swings during the life of the mortgage are not too wild, both lender and borrower benefit from the ARM. If rates go down, the borrower benefits while the lender still makes money. However, if rates rise, the cost to the borrower (subject to the limits agreed upon in the mortgage) *will rise*. In other words, with an ARM the borrower takes the risk if interest rates rise during the life of the mortgage.

If a borrower wants a fixed-rate loan, and some do, a lender must factor the increased exposure to interest rate swings into the rate offered the borrower. Plain and simple, you don't get something for nothing. The borrower who wants the protection of a fixed-rate loan in case interest rates rise will pay a premium for that protection.

ARMs are very prevalent in today's market. Also, other types of consumer credit are often granted on an adjustable rate basis. Many credit cards have variable rates today. Even auto loans can have variable rates now. You need to know about these things.

First-Time Homebuyer Programs

A recent trend in many communities across the nation is "first-time" homebuyer educational programs. When you develop an interest in home ownership, you can sign up for one of these. There is little or no cost involved in enrolling in these programs. They are often sponsored by non-profit community services, sometimes with the government's help. In fact, most Consumer Credit Counseling Services offices conduct first-time homebuyer seminars. In these programs, you get professional advice and valuable information about every aspect of how to choose and finance a home you can afford. In many cases, "graduates" receive financing incentives.

Financing an Automobile

This example may be of more interest to you because, just like Chuck Taylor, you probably will buy a car before you buy a house. The fact that you can save money when you borrow for a shorter term applies to a car loan as well as to a home loan. There are two additional and very important reasons people should go for the shorter loan when buying a car.

The first reason is that a car depreciates. This simply means it starts rapidly losing value the moment you drive it off the lot. If you finance it for too long, the car will be worth less than what you owe on it for about the first three years. This is a potentially dangerous condition. The second reason is that many people don't want to drive the same car for very long. Styles change, cars get better, and many of us just don't want to drive the same car for five or six years.

Financing a car is a big step

In this first example, we keep things simple. There is no trade-in to worry about in these calculations. We're assuming that you have done a good job of bargaining and have gotten a good discount off the "sticker" price. Sales taxes, license and title, and the down payment are typical figures. We also assume you are being smart and have arranged your own insurance on the car.

Negotiated sales price	$18,500
State sales tax (7.3%)	1,350
License and title	150
Less your down payment	(2,000)
Amount to finance	$18,000

Using the Auto Loan Calculator on the Yahoo! web site, we can show how much more the car costs the longer you take to pay for it.

Options for financing the $18,000 at 10 percent simple interest:

Term	Your Monthly Payment	Total Amount Paid	Increase Total Payments Over 36-Month Loan
36 payments	$581.00	$20,909	-0-
48 payments	$457.00	$21,913	+$1,004.00
60 payments	$382.00	$22,946	+$2,037.00

While the monthly payments for the shorter periods are higher, look at how much you save. Financing for five years instead of three adds another $2,037.00 (or about 10 percent) to the cost of the car. It also obligates your future income a lot longer.

There are, however, some other considerations of long-term financing. These things may cost you much more in practical terms than extra interest. Consider the following important points.

- If you financed this car for 36 months, in 18 months you would have it halfway paid for. The balance at that time would be $9,667.00.

- If you financed for 60 months, after 18 payments you still would owe $13,506.00, or about three-fourths of the original amount borrowed.

- If you financed for 36 months and took good care of the car, after 18 payments you probably would have some "equity" in the car, assuming that you took good care of it. That means that the car would be worth more than you owed. If you wanted a nicer car or were just plain tired of driving that one, you could use that equity to "trade up."

If you had financed for 60 months, after 18 payments the car probably would be worth less than the balance owed. You would have "negative" equity. You probably would be married to the car for a very long time, whether you liked it or not.

So you see, while the smaller monthly payments can be attractive, they also can be a dangerous trap. Often it is better to bite the bullet and go for the larger payments.

Leasing an Automobile

These days, many people do not buy a car; rather, they lease one. In fact, more than three out of ten car or truck deals involve a lease instead of a purchase. So, you need to know something about leasing.

Although leasing may provide advantages for some people, an auto lease is, unfortunately, much more complicated than a straight purchase. People who do not completely understand a lease transaction are very likely to be taken advantage of by the companies that lease cars. A lease contract is typically more than three pages long, and it can be filled with a lot of legal terms in fine print. Some of the largest leasing companies are attempting to present the information in a lease agreement more clearly. Nevertheless, you have to be very careful when entering into a lease transaction. Be sure that you understand all of the terms to which you are agreeing.

Basically, when you lease a car or truck, you simply are paying for the *use* of that vehicle for a certain period of time and/or for a certain number of miles. When the term of the lease is over, the vehicle goes back to the leasing company unless you decide to buy it or to lease it again. Because lease agreements are complex, it is often difficult to compare one with another. When you buy a car, it is fairly easy to compare the price from one dealer to another dealer, although financing alternatives can complicate that a bit. Leasing is a different matter.

*Because automobile leases are very complicated, you must
be very careful when entering into a lease transaction*

The big advantage of leasing over purchasing a car is that the monthly payment is lower for the lease. That lower payment lures many people to lease an automobile rather than to buy one.

The big disadvantage is that you are only paying for the use of a car for a limited period of time, such as two or three years. After making monthly payments for all of that time, you have nothing to show for it. But you had use of the car—that's what you paid for.

Many lease contracts also put a limit on the number of miles that you can drive during the lease term. If you drive more miles than allowed, you have to pay a fee per mile. Lease agreements may include an expected value of the car at the end of the lease period. If the value of the car turns out to be less than that amount, you may have to pay the difference. On the other hand, if the value of the car is more than the stated amount, you could get the benefit of that difference. Of course, no one knows for sure today what a car will be worth, say, two or three years from now.

When leasing an automobile, do not focus only on the monthly payment. You have to first consider the vehicle's real selling price. That selling price should not be the list price, but rather a lower negotiated price. When you buy a car, you rarely pay the sticker price that appears on the window of a new car. Rather, you bargain with the dealer to get that price down. In the case of a lease, the lease payment should not be based on the sticker price, but rather on a price that you have negotiated down from the sticker price. That price of the vehicle is called the "capitalized cost." That capitalized cost also may include the license and registration fees.

On most lease deals, you have to make a down payment. That down payment may be in the form of a cash payment or the trade-in of an older vehicle. Any down payment should be subtracted from the capitalized cost. The difference is your "net capitalized cost."

If the dealer guarantees the value of the car at the end of the term of the lease, you would subtract that value from the net capitalized cost. That difference is the amount you are actually financing. It represents the loss of value (depreciation) over the life of the lease.

In addition to paying for the depreciation expected in the value of the vehicle, you also have to pay the leasing company for use of its money during the term of the lease. That payment is called the "lease charge." It is similar to the interest charge on a loan. In addition to the effective interest, some leasing companies will add other fees or expenses to the lease charge.

When you add the lease charge to the amount of the depreciation of the vehicle, you have the total payment. To find out how much you would pay each month, you simply divide that total payment by the number of months of the lease agreement.

To get the best deal in a lease, find out what the capitalized cost of the vehicle is, and try to get the leasing company to tell you about the lease charge. Negotiate with the leasing company on both items.

However, you cannot just compare the monthly payment amounts to determine the best deal. Other parts of the agreement may vary, as well. For example, the term of the lease, the residual value, and the mileage limitation all may be different, and other terms may vary from one lease to another.

When leasing an automobile, you must focus
on the net capitalized cost of the vehicle

It is very important to focus on the net capitalized cost of the vehicle. If you do not know that, you could end up paying much more than necessary over the term of the lease.

Because so many people do not know all they should about leasing, they get the short end of the stick when they lease a vehicle. As with just about everything else in life, the more you know, the better off you are.

Calculation of leasing costs is quite easy using, for example, the lease/buy calculator of the Bloomberg.com web site. Check it out.

Credit Cards—That Fantastic Plastic

What we take for granted today! A person who has established good credit can, when armed with a little piece of plastic, go almost anywhere in the world and use his or her credit. You can get a cash advance on your credit card at almost any ATM, charge a meal, a room, or even a major purchase. Not too many years ago, before powerful computers, these things simply were not possible.

We think Western Union was the first company, in about 1914, to come up with a credit card. It was made of metal. The card was given to special customers allowing them interest-free deferred payments on their business with Western Union. In the 1930s, AT&T introduced a credit card for its customers. But not much else happened in the development of credit cards for a long time.

In the late 1950s, BankAmericard came into being, followed by Master Charge a few years later. Before long, these organizations went global, making these cards useable worldwide. In 1977, BankAmericard changed its name to Visa, to make the name acceptable throughout other countries. Master Charge became MasterCard. The world was never to be the same again.

Both Visa and MasterCard are essentially licensing organizations. They do not issue cards or make the terms. They license banks, credit unions, S&Ls, and other financial institutions to use the name and the networking systems. Each institution is free to set its own terms on the use of the card.

More recently, several other large companies have entered the national and global market, offering their own cards. Some of these are rapidly gaining acceptance as universal credit cards also. Discover is an example of this. A Discover Card is not a MasterCard or Visa, but offers essentially the same product to consumers.

Today, non-financial firms offer Visa and MasterCard by arrangement with a lender. Examples are Exxon and General Motors, which enable you to earn discounts on their products as you use their credit cards.

When we talk about credit cards, we just may be talking about the most popular and most valued consumer product, or convenience, ever created. We are talking about big business! To give you some idea of what is going on in the world of credit cards, in 1998 consumers charged almost *$1.4 trillion* on Visa cards alone! In that year there were over 800 million Visa cards in circulation. Remember also that these numbers we just gave you do not include MasterCard, Discover Card, American Express, or any of the thousands of retail cards being used, such as Sears, Montgomery Wards, or J. C. Penny.

If you were to lay end-to-end the 800 million Visa cards in circulation at the present time, they would stretch almost 44,000 miles! That's the distance from New York to Egypt—and back—four times!

Now, with any of the several cards offered, you can shop or travel almost anywhere, get cash out of your bank account from thousands of locations, and much more. You get one monthly bill, detailing all of your charges. You can pay the bill in full, often without any interest, or make smaller payments over a period of time (with interest). That can be a trap or a tool, depending on your discipline and management ability.

Getting a Credit Card

One of the most intense and competitive marketing campaigns in our history has been going on for the last several years. All across America mailboxes are full of credit card solicitations. Many credit card companies are focusing their selling efforts on young adults, particularly college students. So, when you are ready to apply for your first credit card, you will not have to look very hard to find a credit card application.

To get a piece of the fantastic plastic, you apply to the card company of your choice. The company checks your credit and determines your capacity. Then it gives you a credit limit and issues you the card. Each card company has its specific terms, governed in certain ways by federal law (we talk about terms a little later). So long as you do not exceed your charge limit, do not abuse the privilege of using credit, and live up to the payment terms, you can enjoy the wonderful world of plastic.

When you use the card, here is what generally happens This varies somewhat according to where you use the card. Because even more changes in automation are taking place, not every merchant has the same tools yet.

In a fully automated environment, the clerk rings up your sale. Then, you or the clerk takes your card and zips it through a small scanner. Then, electronics take over. In just a few seconds, the machine reads the magnetic stripe on your card, calls a computer somewhere else in the world, and tells that computer about your purchase and everything else it needs to know to check your account. At this point, and in a fraction of a second, computers check your paying habits and the expiration date of your card. The computer even compares the amount of the purchase with the typical purchase you make, and it compares where the transaction is occurring with where your transactions usually take place. The charge then is compared against your balance and credit limit. In another few seconds, the clerk's computerized register receives the approval, prints your charge ticket which you sign, and the deal is done. Your account has been charged and the merchant's account will be credited, all with tiny electrical impulses sent over wires or optical fibers at the speed of light. Because the process is so highly automated, it costs very little and is incredibly fast.

If you are in Paris, France, and use your American Express Card, the approval involves a 46,000-mile electronic journey over telephone lines and through computers!

The same card can be popped into an automated teller machine known as an ATM. You can inquire about your account or get cash to go out on the town. To use an ATM, you need a PIN, or Personal Identification Number. That number comes from the issuer of your card. Never write down your PIN number. You don't want a thief to get your number and steal your money. When you insert your card in an ATM, the machine will ask you for your PIN. That number is matched up with your card. If correct, the machine will allow you to get money out of your account or to check your balance.

Like any form of credit, the plastic kind can be a powerful tool. But for many people, credit cards can be a little harder to manage wisely. The cards require a higher degree of self-discipline. After all, they can be like carrying around a large supply of cash—cash you may not have. Many good and honest people who can manage other forms of credit get into trouble with credit cards. The cards are so easy to use. Most people quickly learn their lesson, get back on course, and are the wiser. But a few should avoid credit cards entirely. They just cannot resist the impulse buying that credit cards can make possible. Remember this when you get your first card.

If you apply for and receive a credit card, do not allow yourself to be a victim of fraud. Keep your credit card number private. Do not leave your statements, or anything with your account number on it, laying around. Never give your credit card number, or any other number such as your checking account number, to someone who calls you on the phone. Even if they have a good-sounding story about why they need your number, it may be a scam. You will wind up with charges on your next statement that you know nothing about.

Remember also, not all cards are the same. Each can have different interest rates and other terms. Some states severely limit interest rates card companies can charge. Others permit much higher rates. We have seen rates vary from 9.9 to 23.99 percent on the unpaid balance. In addition, there can be heavy charges if the account balance goes over the authorized credit limit. Usually, there will also be extra charges for late payments. Many card agreements provide for no interest if the balance is paid in full each month.

This is called a "grace period." You should check for this feature when shopping for a credit card.

In all cases, federal law requires each company to give you a written statement of all the terms of its cards. Many people don't take the time to check out this information. We hope you will not be one of these.

You might think we would be better off if the government required that interest rates be very low. This is not true. If rates were so low that these companies could not make a profit, this fantastic plastic would not be available for us.

The "Secured Card"

In recent years there has been a product marketed for people who cannot qualify for a true credit card. This is called a "secured card." We mentioned the secured card in Chapter 7. A secured card is similar to a true credit card, but it must be secured by an actual savings deposit. You open a savings account with, say, $400, and you get a secured card with, typically, a $400 limit. You are paid interest on the savings, but of course you pay a much higher rate of interest for the use of the card. You really are paying for using your own money.

About the only good thing about these cards is that it is possible for people to establish credit with them, and later get a true credit card.

Remember that credit cards are but one form of consumer credit. They may be the most modern, they may be the most talked about, and they may appear to be very desirable. Properly used, with budgeting and discipline, they are all of these things and more. But for many people, credit cards are the most difficult form of credit to manage. That is because credit cards are so very convenient to use. Credit cards are not for everyone. Some people are better off using installment credit to obtain the better things in life (that they can afford). Installment credit has certain checks and balances against overuse. You must think about what you want to use installment credit for and why, and then arrange a loan for a specific amount of money for a specific length of time. It is much more difficult to make bad mistakes in judgment using installment credit than it is using a credit card.

THINGS TO REMEMBER

Interest is the price you pay for the use of someone else's money.

The amount of interest you pay is determined by: (1) the interest rate, (2) the amount of money involved, and (3) how long you use the money.

The only way a lender or retailer can make credit available is to charge interest.

Almost any contract will provide for late charges if the terms of the agreement are not kept. The *Disclosure Statement* will advise you of all costs or fees.

The "term" of a loan governs how fast you pay the money back. Paying back credit rapidly not only saves you interest, but regains your credit capacity that much quicker.

Collateral is property—anything of value—that the borrower pledges to the lender to reduce the lender's risk.

A person who has built a good credit record and has good income often can borrow without collateral.

The *Credit Application* is what gives the lender most of the information required. If that information meets a lender's basic credit policies, a credit report may be ordered from one or more credit bureaus to determine if that person has a history of satisfactory repayment.

The use of credit cards requires a high degree of management and discipline. Installment credit, or personal loans, are a more manageable form of credit for some people.

Protect your credit card numbers. Never give anyone who calls you your credit card number. You may wind up a victim of fraud.

The Internet can be used to shop for loans as well as to make calculations related to loans and leases.

Chapter Ten

All About Credit Bureaus

After Chuck filled in his credit application to finance his car, the lender saw that Chuck might be a good candidate for a loan. Of course, the lender needed more information about Chuck and his credit history before he could actually consider approving the loan. The lender knew that Chuck was young and would not have a long credit history, but it was necessary to check that Chuck did not have a bad record. So, the lender contacted a credit bureau.

When you have finished this chapter, you will fully understand the important role credit bureaus *will* play in your life. You will understand how they compile information about you. You will see how they make that information available to creditors you wish to do business with. You will learn how they help responsible consumers get credit by maintaining records of their good paying habits. You also will learn how credit bureaus help businesses that extend credit avoid making mistakes by *not* advancing credit to people who don't have a good record of paying debts.

Consider these facts:

- There are over *190 million* active credit files in the U.S. today.

- Every year credit bureaus in the U.S. issue about *one billion* credit reports. This number has almost doubled in the past five years.

- Americans with good credit enjoy the privilege of using more than *$1.3 trillion* in consumer installment credit each year, and another $583 billion in revolving debt. This doesn't include credit to purchase homes! Furthermore, there exists approximately $2 trillion in approved, but unused, credit lines!

To help you understand the last bullet, here's an example of an *unused credit line*. Were you to apply for a credit card and be approved, the issuer may, for example, set a $2,000 limit. This means that you may charge up to that amount. If you were to charge $500, you would have $1,500 unused in your line of credit. Another important example is the case of a homeowner who wants a credit line secured by the equity in his or her home. If a person has, say, $20,000 in equity in his or her home (equity is the difference between the value of the home and the mortgage balance still owed), the individual might be granted a $10,000 line of credit. Any part of that credit line that is not used represents an unused, or available, line of credit.

There are three major credit reporting companies in the U.S.—Equifax Credit Information Services, Trans Union Corporation, and Experian. Each of these companies owns many individual credit bureaus, and each makes its files available to other, independently owned credit bureaus. All of the big three, and most other credit bureaus, are members of Associated Credit Bureaus, Inc., an international trade association. These members follow a stringent Code of Ethics. These ethics are carefully designed to benefit and protect the public.

Here are the addresses and phone numbers of the three major credit reporting companies:

Equifax—P.O Box 740256, Atlanta, GA 30374. Toll-free, 1-800-685-1111

Experian—P.O. Box 9530, Allen, TX 75013. Toll-free, 1-800-422-4879

Trans Union—P.O. Box 390, Springfield, PA 19064. Toll-free, 1-800-256-1902

What Is a Credit Bureau?

A credit bureau is a "credit reporting agency." That is the legal definition. Actually, a credit bureau is simply a company that gathers information on people who use credit. Credit bureaus sell that information to companies that grant credit. That information is called a "credit report." A credit bureau also may furnish a report to an employer to whom you apply for a job, or even to a prospective landlord whose apartment you want to rent. It will also supply information to many other legitimate kinds of inquirers who want to do business with you.

Where Does a Credit Bureau Get Its Information About You?

The information in a credit report is gathered from a number of sources. The information is usually referred to as "data." Most of the data come from creditors with whom you do business. Other data come from public records. If someone sues you—files a lawsuit claiming you owe him or her money—that information is public record. If you file for bankruptcy, that also is public record. It is on file at a courthouse for the world to see. Credit bureaus also pass data to other credit bureaus. If you move, your credit record follows you. You can run, but you can't hide!

What Information Is in Your Credit Report?

Study the two sample credit reports in this section. One is that of a 21 year-old, off to a good start using credit wisely and building credit ratings. The other person, also young, obviously has had problems. Which would you lend money to?

Credit reports contain a lot of information. First, there is identification and employment data. This includes your name and address, your employer, your Social Security number, and maybe even your birthday. Other information, such as how long you've lived in the same place and whether or not you are a job-hopper, is of value to a creditor. After all that dull stuff comes the meat. A lot of information is tracked on your credit history. When did you start doing business? Whom have you done business with? What was the date of your last payment? How much credit was extended to you? How much do you owe now? Do you keep your word and pay on time? These companies, and the creditors who pay for the information, are only interested in information that may affect your financial stability. They don't care about your social life or how you wear your hair.

Why Do We Have Credit Bureaus?

It's very simple. People need credit, and companies can't extend credit without good information about which applicants are deadbeats and which applicants pay their bills on time. A hundred years ago, people couldn't get credit the way we do today. Back then, a farmer could go to the local bank and make a loan to buy seed. He paid for it when the crop came in. But the guy at the bank knew the farmer, knew his reputation, and knew he wasn't going to run off anywhere. Big companies or large landowners could get credit because they had collateral. The rest of us who were not well known were out of luck. However, we didn't need credit then, because those cars and TVs were not available to buy! Now, credit makes the world go around. We need credit bureaus to collect and make available the information necessary to have credit transactions.

How to Find Out About Your Credit Report

Your credit bureau record probably will get started the first time you apply for credit. There won't be much information on file at first. Your data will grow as you build a credit history. There are some very important things you need to know. Suppose you are denied credit because of information in a credit bureau file. The creditor is required

CREDIT BUREAU OF ZZZZ
P.O. BOX 345
ANY TOWN, USA

(222) 555-2600

JOHN ALLAN DOE
342 OAK ALLEY
MAIN TOWN, AL

DATE 11/15/00
SOCIAL SECURITY NUMBER 022-28-1852
DATE OF BIRTH 01/01/79

CREDIT HISTORY

Company Name	Account Number	Whose Acct.	Date Opened	Months Reviewed	Date Of Last Activity	High Credit	Terms	All Items as of Date Reported			Date Reported
								Balance	Past Due	Status	
Any Bank	123456	I	05/00	05	10/00	1205	55	930	0	I1	10/00
Good Jewelry	2345678	I	06/99	12	09/00	375	35	35	0	R1	10/00
Home Furniture Company	33333	J	03/00		10/00	400	40	120	0	I1	10/00
Town Department Store	1234-456-33333	I	08/99	10	06/00	300	25	0	0	R1	08/00
Bankcard	4567-4332568953-33	J	07/99		10/00	1000	20	100	0	R1	10/00

Amount in H/C Column is Credit Limit

******************************Additional Information*****************************
>>>>>Former/Other Address Box 536, Any Town
>>>>>Last Reported Employment Management Trainee, XYZ Corp.
>>>>>Former/Other Employment Part-Time, Stoney Point Pizza
*************Companies That Requested Your Credit History********************

06/02/00	DISCLOSURE	12/20/99	PR J.R.'s Easy Finance
03/22/00	Home Furniture Company	06/02/99	Good Jewelry
07/01/00	AR Bankcard	08/13/99	Town Department Store

THE FOLLOWING INQUIRIES ARE **NOT** REPORTED TO BUSINESSES:

PRM – This type of inquiry means that only your name and address were given to a credit grantor so they could offer you an application for credit. (PRM inquiries may remain for up to 12 months.)

AM or **AR** – These inquiries indicate a periodic review of your credit history by one of your creditors. (AM and AR inquires may remain for up to 12 months.)

DISCLOSURE, ACIS, or **UPDATE** – These inquiries indicate our activity in response to your contact with us for either a copy of your credit file or a request for research.

PRM, AM, AR, DISCLOSURE, ACIS and **UPDATE** inquiries do not show on credit files that businesses receive, only on copies provided to you.

ACCOUNT STATUS

TYPE OF ACCOUNT:

Open (entire balance due each month)	O
Revolving	R
Installment (fixed number of payments)	I

CURRENT MANNER OF PAYMENT
(Using Payments Past Due or Age from Due Date)

	TYPE OF ACCOUNT		
	O	R	I
Too new to rate; approved but not used	0	0	0
Paid as agreed	1	1	1
30+ days past due	2	2	2
60+ days past due	3	3	3
90+ days past due	4	4	4
Pays (or paid) 120+ days past the due date; or collection account	5	5	5
Making regular payments under wage earner plan or similar arrangement	7	7	7
Repossession	8	8	8
Charged off to bad debt	9	9	9

◆ **SAMPLE CREDIT REPORT** ◆

JOHN Q. FOX
1677 MAIN STREET
ANY TOWN, USA

DATE 11/15/00
SOCIAL SECURITY NUMBER 078-05-1120
DATE OF BIRTH 01/01/76

Please address all future ➡
correspondence to this address

CREDIT BUREAU OF XXXXX
P.O. BOX 123
ANY TOWN, USA
(444) 555-7575

CREDIT HISTORY

Company Name	Account Number	Whose Acct.	Date Opened	Months Reviewed	Date Of Last Activity	High Credit	Terms	Balance	Past Due	Status	Date Reported
XYZ Bank	987654	I	05/96		01/98	2000	75	1400	1400	I9	05/99
	Charged Off Account										
Good Jewelry	5693678	I	04/96	12	06/98	600	50	550	550	R9	10/00
	Charged Off Account										
Sam's Furniture	23890	I	03/97		02/98	900	45	675	675	I9	10/00
Corner Department Store	2386-555-55893	I	08/96	10	06/98	300	25	250	250	R9	08/00
	Charged Off Account										
Bankcard	4599-46987-5681-21	I	07/97		09/98	2000	40	1675	1675	R9	10/00
	Charged Off Account										

Amount in H/C Column is Credit Limit

Note: "All Items as of Date Reported" spans Balance, Past Due, Status columns.

************************************Courthouse Records*********************************
>>>>>Bankruptcy Filed 08/98 Case Number 345723
>>>>>Judgement Filed 06/98 City Court Case Number 456733 Defendant John Doe, Amount $300
>>>>>Lien Filed 12/99 Amount $4250, Class Federal
************************************Additional Information*****************************
>>>>>Former/Other Address 1256 Morning Street, Kansas City Kansas
>>>>>Former/Other Address Rt 2 Box 345, Dallas Texas
>>>>>Former/Other Address 12346 Willow Street, Baltimore MD
>>>>>Last Reported Employment Laborer, Bullet Construction Company
>>>>>Former/Other Employment Carpenter Helper, Wild's Building Company
>>>>>Former/Other Employment Routsabout, Baytown Marine
*********************Companies That Requested Your Credit History*********************
06/15/99 Any Bank   06/02/99 Cornerstone Furniture
03/12/90 Home Furniture Company 07/01/99 Corner Bank and Trust
07/10/99 Auto Finance Company   07/11/99 Jim's Auto Sales
07/01/00 Bankcard

EXPLANATION OF CODED INFORMATION

WHOSE ACCOUNT
Indicates who is responsible for the account and the type of participation you have with the account.

J — Joint
I — Individual
U — Undesignated
A — Authorized User
T — Terminated
M — Maker
C — Co-Maker/Co-Signer
B — On Behalf of another person
S — Shared

by law to notify you of the name, address and phone number of the credit bureau that supplied any information to it. If you contact that credit bureau within 60 days to learn what is in your credit file, you are entitled to that information at no charge.

There are three other circumstances under which you may obtain a free copy of your credit report. One is if you are unemployed and plan to look for a job within the next two months. The second is if you are on welfare. Finally, in the case where your report is inaccurate because of fraud. In these cases, you may obtain one free copy in a year's time.

You are entitled to learn what is in your file at any other time. There will be a small charge of about $8. The yellow pages of the telephone book will tell you the name (or names) of the credit bureaus in your area. Call and find out the rules. Credit bureau representatives won't tell you about your report on the phone. When you properly identify yourself, they may mail you a copy or make an appointment for you to come in and see your report. Most cities have two and sometimes three credit bureaus. Several are very large national companies with hundreds of offices. That competition makes credit bureaus work harder to collect more and accurate data. Competition also keeps prices down by avoiding a monopoly.

What if Your Credit Report Is Wrong?

Most credit reports are very accurate. This is largely the result of competition. If a credit bureau gets a reputation for producing wrong information, creditors won't pay for that bureau's reports. It will go out of business. However, errors can happen.

We recommend that you check your report every two years. Many experts recommend every year. If you find any wrong information in your file, the law gives you the right to get it corrected without charge. If you discover incorrect information, the credit bureau must recheck the source and correct the information if it is wrong. If the information is on somebody else, the credit bureau must remove it. If the information cannot be verified, the credit bureau also must remove it.

There can be what is called an omission. This is when you may have some good credit that simply isn't in your file. The law does not require a credit bureau to have everything. But for a small fee most credit bureaus will "update" your report. The credit bureau will check your references and include that data in your report.

What if You Have Derogatory Information in Your Report?

If that information is accurate, tough luck! You get what you earn. If you have earned a good credit file by paying your bills on time, you enjoy the rewards. If you have been irresponsible, you pay the price for that by having a bad credit report.

There is a provision designed to help anyone who incurs a derogatory rating due to an offsetting circumstance. The Fair Credit Reporting Act provides that a consumer may place a message of 100 words or less in his or her credit report. This can be very helpful if there is a dispute about a debt. It may also be helpful if there were temporary problems, such as unemployment, that caused a poor rating in an otherwise good report.

Negative information, often referred to as "derogatory," that is correct cannot be removed from your file. There is nothing you or anyone else can do to force a credit bureau to remove information that is accurate. So-called "credit doctors" or "credit repair services" may claim to be able to remove bad information from your file. Only a dummy believes that he or she can get good credit when it is not deserved.

Derogatory information can include judgments, liens, accounts turned over to collection agencies, charge-offs, late payments, and repossessions. It also includes, of course, that financial failure called bankruptcy.

Most of the time, bad credit ratings are well deserved. Sometimes, however, people can get into trouble through problems they can't help. Loss of income and poor health are just two of the uncertainties we all face in life. If individuals haven't used too much credit and if they have some savings, they should be able to weather a little storm without it raining on their credit. When good, honest folks get into credit trouble, there's hope. If the problem is too much debt, non-profit counseling agencies such as Consumer Credit Counseling Services can help by getting creditors to cooperate with a common-sense repayment plan. Even if the problem is simply self-discipline or personal management, these agencies often can help through counseling. If a person faces problems squarely, gets on a strict budget, and avoids using credit for a while, with a little sacrifice the debts will get paid. That person's credit report will begin to improve again.

How Long Can Derogatory Information Remain on File?

The Fair Credit Reporting Act also governs how long bad credit stays on a report. Most of it stays for seven years.

But there are important exceptions. A bankruptcy can stay on for 10 years! And there are three circumstances where a bankruptcy can be reported forever. They are when someone (1) applies for credit in an amount larger than $150,000; (2) applies for a life insurance policy of $150,000 or more; or (3) applies for a job that pays $75,000 or more and the employer gets a credit report in connection with the job application. Obviously, bad credit can affect your chances of getting a job. Many employers get credit reports on applicants. Would you want somebody who doesn't pay his or her bills working for you?

Credit Repair Clinics

In recent years, somebody figured out a new way to make money from ignorant or lazy people. Credit repair companies claim they can "fix" or "clean up" or "repair" bad credit. We've already told you that nobody can make a credit bureau remove bad ratings if they are correct! The Fair Credit Reporting Act gives you the right to have any incorrect information corrected or removed *FREE!* The Federal Trade Commission has issued many warnings to the public about "credit repair" companies and some of the things they claim to do. Only an ignorant or lazy person is going to pay one of these companies hundreds of dollars and more to do it for him or her. Remember, a fool and his money are soon parted.

In summary, a good credit rating will prove to be among the most valuable assets you may ever earn. We say "earn" because that's the only way to have and maintain a good credit rating. Earning a good credit rating will require you to learn how to get and keep a job so that you can produce income, to practice good money management skills, and to develop self-discipline so that you use only the credit you can afford.

THINGS TO REMEMBER

A credit bureau is a company that gathers information on people who use credit. A credit bureau then sells this information to creditors needing the data to make good credit decisions. This information can also be supplied to others for legitimate purposes, such as employment decisions or landlord-lessee decisions.

A credit bureau gathers information primarily from companies you do business with and from public records.

A credit report contains data such as whom you owe, how much you owe those creditors, and how you have paid your bills. It can contain other information such as employment.

The Fair Credit Reporting Act gives you the right to find out what is contained in your credit report. If you are turned down for credit, that same law requires the creditor to tell you which credit bureau supplied the information on which the decision was based.

If your credit report contains inaccurate information, there is a good, workable process whereby you may get the information corrected.

If a person has not paid his or her bills promptly, as agreed, there is no legal way to get bad ratings off the record. Bad ratings are the price of not paying accounts properly. Derogatory information, such as paying slowly, can stay on a record for seven years. A bankruptcy filing can remain for 10 years.

There are CCCS offices all across the country. They usually can help the honest person in trouble get back on his or her feet and on the way to a good financial future. Like shopping for any goods or service, however, you should check out any company before using it.

Never sign anything or pay a fee to anyone who tells you he or she can get bad ratings removed from your credit report. If negative information is accurate, you are stuck with it.

Chapter Eleven

Making a Checking Account Work for You

When Chuck Taylor got his first part-time job several years ago, he opened a checking account at a nearby bank. Having the account was convenient for him, and he knew the bank was a safe place to keep his money. Also, Chuck found that he made good contacts at the bank—people who had an interest in him later when he wanted that car loan.

As Chuck discovered, there is a lot to know about checking accounts. And it's all-important because a checking account, properly used, is a building block of good money management.

All About Checking Accounts
Everybody knows what a checking account is and how it is used. Can you imagine life without this simple but

powerful tool? Imagine your parents or your teacher carrying around all of their cash. Or, imagine them first driving to the bank to get money out of an account every time they went to the store. Imagine business people carrying around suitcases full of cash to close a deal. If there were no checking accounts, all business activity would grind to a slow crawl.

Today you can get a checking account at a commercial bank, a credit union, or a savings and loan association or at other types of thrift institutions such as federal savings banks. You can write checks against accounts at some money market mutual funds, too.

In addition to writing checks against your checking account to pay for something, you can use a computer to transfer money out of your account at some banks. Electronic bill-paying is increasing rapidly in popularity as it is more convenient, cheaper (no postage to pay), and secure (no paper checks that can be lost or forged).

Unless you keep a large amount of money in a checking account, you will pay service charges that reflect the cost of providing you the service. These service charges can vary widely from institution to institution. On top of that, most institutions offer several different types of accounts so that you can choose the one that best fits your needs. You must learn how to shop for services. You need to recognize those services that are best for you.

Choosing an Account

It is easy to choose the kind of account you want. And it is easy to pick a bank, credit union, or savings and loan. If members of your family do business at the Corner Bank and are happy with the service there, that bank would be a good choice for you. Just stop by the office and tell someone that you wish to open a checking account. If you are neat and your hair isn't three colors, you should get a nice welcome. When you sit down with a bank officer, ask him or her to explain the options. There are several kinds of checking accounts.

The Kinds of Accounts

We can't tell you about all the different accounts you will be offered in a rapidly changing market, but we can mention a few general types. For example, there probably will be an account that is free if you keep a minimum balance of, say, $500.

If you are not able to maintain a high balance, banks usually offer an account with a very small monthly charge, typically two or three dollars a month. With this account, you usually are limited to a certain number of checks (maybe 20) a month. With this account, you would not be required to keep a minimum balance.

Let's hope you don't turn out to be one of those people who write checks at the local convenience store for two dollars! It is a source of amazement to us (and profit to the people who print checks) as to why some people insist on writing ridiculous numbers of small checks every month. Cash does have its place.

You can get money out of your checking account by using an ATM (Automated Teller Machine). Some accounts may limit the number of free teller or ATM transactions you can have each month. After that number, the bank will charge you. The charge may range from a quarter to a dollar or more for each transaction.

There are many institutions that offer free accounts to students in high school and college. You should definitely check out this possibility if you qualify.

Other Costs and Charges

Chuck learned that almost all accounts involve a charge for printed checks. Most banks have plain, low-cost checks and also very expensive, fancy checks. It may make you feel good to write checks printed with beautiful scenes. But you are going to pay extra for those checks. That's your choice to make.

You should also ask if it costs extra to have your driver's license number, phone number, and other information printed on the checks. You may not want all this information printed on your checks. However, most merchants are going to ask you for it anyway when you use your checks.

Of course, electronic payments do not involve paper checks. So, you save when you do not use traditional checks. However, you would still use paper checks at least from time to time even with an Internet deposit account. Select your checks carefully.

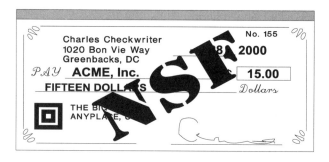

NSF (Non-Sufficient Funds) Checks

You are going to be charged if you write checks without having enough money in your account to cover them. That charge will probably be $18 or more. You must not misuse your account and let this happen to you. You see, writing an NSF check can cost you a lot more than the institution's charge. It can become a source of serious trouble.

A bank has two choices when you write an NSF check. It can return (bounce) the check to the person or business firm that deposited it, or it can pay the check as a courtesy to you. Or, the bank can pay the check if the shortage is not too large. This is called an overdraft. Either way, you will pay a charge. Your bank will be more likely to pay (overdraft) an accidental NSF check if you do not have a history of writing NSF checks. The institution is not under any obligation to pay a bad check, not even for one penny! You are not supposed to write an NSF check, period. Under certain circumstances, if you write a bad check, you may violate a criminal law.

Whether the bank pays or bounces the check, you will be sent a notice advising you of the action. The notice will tell you the amount of the charge (the institution's fee) for the bad check your wrote. You should subtract the amount of that charge from your account balance in your stubs, or check record, right then; otherwise, you may forget it. That could cause you even more embarrassment and expense later.

If your bank returns the check to the merchant who deposited it, you will have messed up the merchant's account with his or her bank. This is because that merchant's bank will charge the merchant's account for the worthless deposit. The merchant made a deposit expecting your check to be honored. If one of your checks should be returned, contact the merchant immediately.

If you know for a fact that you have straightened out the problem in your account, you may ask the merchant to re-deposit the check. However, the merchant instead may require you to come by and make the check good in cash. You also may have to pay the merchant a fee up to $25 for having caused the trouble. If this is the case, do so immediately. Don't forget—the merchant took your check fully expecting it to be good.

If you have written several bad checks, your problems are multiplied. In any case, find out what happened. If an error was made in your account, straighten it out. If you cannot understand immediately what the problem is, call your bank. Ask for an appointment to see someone for help. Someone will sit down with you and help you figure out what has happened and how to straighten things out. Above all, remember that you must communicate. The worst thing you can do is to do nothing. Take the initiative to make things right.

How to Avoid Messing up Your Checking Account

Chuck Taylor found out the hard way that you could mess up your account by failing to enter the amount in the stubs immediately after writing a check. He once found a check missing from his book. It wasn't really missing! The amount of the check and whom he paid with it were not entered in the stubs. He remembered writing the check but could not remember how much the check was for. He was a little embarrassed, but he called the store where he wrote it. The clerk was nice enough to look it up. The next time you write a check, see how long it takes to properly and completely record the transaction in your checkbook. It's probably not more than eight seconds. In Chuck's case, he learned a lesson without doing harm. Because he was not constantly drawing his bank account down to a low balance, he had enough money in the bank to cover his mistake.

Also, you can mess up your account by not promptly balancing, or reconciling, your checkbook when the bank statement comes in or when you call it up on your computer screen. The reason it is so important to balance your

You should balance your checkbook promtply
to avoid costly and embarrassing errors

checking account promptly each month is that you will, sooner or later, make simple errors during the month. On very rare occasions, the bank employees make mistakes. Without prompt balancing, these errors will be undetected. Several small errors may pile up, or you may make one big error, and before you know it you have problems. Keeping good account records is more important than ever before because today many banks do not send cancelled checks back to you in your monthly bank statement. So, keep your check register accurately as you go through each month.

Balancing your checkbook really is easy and quick—once you learn how. And, learning how is easy also! Next, we explain a few basic, but important, terms you need to know. Then, we show you how easy it is to keep a checkbook straight.

Outstanding Check(s)

This term refers to one or more checks that you have written but which have not yet been paid against your account at your bank. Usually a check will clear promptly. However, it is not unusual for a check to take up to a week or more to reach your bank. If you handle your account right by entering and subtracting checks in your checkbook or check register when you write them, outstanding checks will never cause you a problem. The only time you even need to know anything about outstanding checks is when you reconcile (balance) your checkbook with your bank statement.

Reconciling Item

This term refers to an item other than a check that must be taken into account when you balance your checkbook. Such items must be recorded and entered into your checkbook. A reconciling item usually will be a service charge, a charge for printed checks, interest the bank has paid you, or something similar.

Transit Item

A transit item is a deposit that you have made but which has not yet been posted to your bank account. It is said to be "in transit." Remember this: If your deposit has not been posted to your account or if the money has not yet been collected by the bank (if the deposit was a check or a money order) your money is not there for you to use. In other words, don't write checks before your deposit gets to the bank and has time to be credited to your account! Your institution will tell you its rules. Some institutions "cut off" transactions at 2:00 p.m. All transactions after that time are posted to accounts the next day. If you deposit by mail, allow time for your deposit to be received and posted. When it comes time to reconcile your statement, you may have to consider a "deposit in transit."

Availability of Funds

This term refers to a delay your bank may impose on your access to funds when you deposit checks drawn against another institution. For example, suppose for your birthday Grandma sends you a check drawn on Another State Bank and Trust located in Grandma's hometown. After you deposit it, you should allow a few days for it to clear before you try to cash one of your own checks. After all, you can't expect your bank to pay out money before it gets the money from Grandma's bank! If you have a job that pays with an out-of-state check, it might be a good idea to ask your institution what the clearing time is. A federal law specifies how long an institution can wait before making your funds available to you. There is information on display at the bank or other institution giving you details.

Overdraft

An overdraft is created when you write a check for which you do not have enough money in your account, and the bank decides to honor your check. You are now "overdrawn." The bank has shown you a courtesy by honoring the check. The bank is not under any obligation to pay on your NSF check. Frankly, most banks will not even consider that unless you have a good record. If you write NSF checks too often, that good record will be lost. Even if the bank does honor your check, there will be a charge for the service. As in the case of any charge, you must enter it in your stubs or your account will be out of balance.

If you have a credit card with the bank, you can set up "overdraft privileges." This arrangement covers an NSF check by charging your credit card and putting the money in your checking account to clear the check. Usually, however, the minimum amount the bank will charge your credit card is $100. This is true even if you were short only a few dollars in your checking account. Of course, you pay a fee for this service. It may be a good idea to have this feature, just in case you make an honest mistake in your checking account. But, if you get sloppy with your account, or just use the feature too often, it can get expensive.

Endorsements and Other Details

Any check you deposit must have been drawn (written) properly and endorsed (signed on the back) correctly. The numeric and written amounts on the front of the check must agree, and the signature must be correct. Also, you must endorse it on the back exactly as it was made out. In other words, if Chuck received a check made payable to C. W. Taylor, Chuck must sign it on the back "C. W. Taylor."

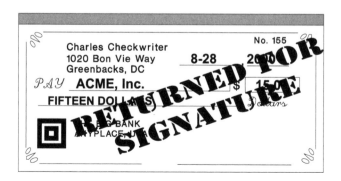

There are a few other details you need to learn to avoid trouble. The most important is that you are fully responsible for any checks that you deposit into your account. In other words, if you deposit a check that bounces, the bank is going to charge your account for it. The check will be mailed back to you with an explanation. It's not the institution's job to collect it for you. Your gripe is with whoever gave you the check, not with the bank. Common sense and acceptance of responsibility will enable you to avoid most problems.

Reading Your Bank Statement

Your bank statement is a monthly summary of activity that the institution has posted to your account. It is very important that you learn how to read your bank statement. It really isn't hard. Statements from different banks may not look alike, but they all show the same things. Many banks make your bank statement available to you daily. You just access it electronically on your computer.

First, look at the summary information. It starts with your beginning balance for the one-month period. It shows the total of deposits that the institution has received during the month (credits), the total of checks and electronic transfers charged against your account for the month (debits), and finally, the ending balance. The service charge is a debit, but usually it is stated separately.

Next, look at the detail. This is a listing of each individual deposit made and each check and electronic charge that has cleared your account. If there have been any adjustments to your account, they too will be listed. They are often labeled as "debit memos" or "credit memos." The checks usually will be listed in the order of the check numbers. This will not necessarily be the same order in which they were paid.

There is a very important thing to remember when reading your statement. The statement shows a month of activity affecting the institution. It will seldom agree with the activity in your checkbook. This is because of the time it takes checks to clear your account. On occasion, there may be a deposit in transit. But don't worry about this now. It will all be very clear when you reconcile your checkbook with the bank statement. Never change your checkbook until you have reconciled it with the bank and positively identified any reason for change.

Reconciling Your Checkbook

Reconciling your checkbook involves proving that your records agree with the bank statement. It consists of a few steps and simple math. Follow along, referring to the illustrations on pages 146–149, and you will see how easy it is. We assume you are starting with the first monthly statement on a new account or one that was in balance the prior month.

Your bank statement probably will have a fill-in-the-blanks form printed on the back to help you balance, as does the one in the illustration. We show you a little short cut. It is the same process, but will save you some time and writing.

Step One—Identify the Paid Checks

This is easy. The real purpose is not so much to identify the paid checks as to pin down the "outstanding" ones. Somewhere in your checkbook stubs there will be a margin or an unused column where you can make a mark or an X. First, look at your bank statement to see which checks have been listed (paid). Next, make a small mark in your checkbook for each of your checks that have cleared the bank. Third, make a list of those checks that you have written but which are not listed on your statement. Include all of them right up to the last one you wrote. Add them up and jot down the total. If you are using the form on the

ANY TOWN BANK
P.O. BOX 9999
ANY TOWN, USA 70000
(800) 555-5555

JULY   23, 2000
ACCOUNT #100000000000

MEMBER FDIC

MR. JOHN Q. DOE
1234 ANY STREET
ANY TOWN, USA 70000-0000

BALANCE LAST STATEMENT	DEPOSITS & CREDITS		CHECKS & WITHDRAWALS		SERVICE CHARGE	BALANCE THIS STATEMENT
	NO.	TOTAL AMOUNT	NO.	TOTAL AMOUNT		
75.00	3	470.00	7	180.40	7.OO	357.60

CLUB ACCOUNT   ACCOUNT #100000000000

U.S. SAVINGS BONDS ARE TAX-FREE FOR EDUCATION. IT'S SMARTER THAN EVER
TO START SAVING TODAY.

DEPOSITS AND NON-CHECK TRANSACTIONS

7/01	225.00	Deposit	
7/15	225.00	Deposit	
7/15	20.00	ATM Deposit	
7/21	22.50	ATM Service Charge	
7/31	1.00	Maintenance Fee	OD Protection
7/31	7.00	Service Charge	

CHECKS CLEARED THIS MONTH

DATE	CHECK NO.	AMOUNT	DATE	CHECK NO.	AMOUNT
7/13	540	65.00	7/14	542	37.25
7/15	543	20.00	7/18	544	34.65

THIS FORM IS PROVIDED TO HELP YOU
RECONCILE YOUR CHECKING ACCOUNT

CHECKS OUTSTANDING
(Those written which have
not cleared the bank)

NO.	$
TOTAL	$

(1) BANK BALANCE
   Shown on this
   statement $ _____

(2) ADD (If Any)
   Deposits not shown
   on this statement   _____

(3) TOTAL $ _____

(4) SUBTRACT
   Outstanding checks _____

(5) BALANCE (Should
   agree with your
   checkbook balance) $ _____

This balance should agree with your
checkbook balance after deducting charges
(if any) and adding any interest earned as
shown on this statement.

If you have any questions or problems
related to this statement or any of your bank
accounts, please contact the branch where
you do business. Your personal banker will
be pleased to be of assistance.

NUMBER	DATE	TRANSACTION DESCRIPTION	PAYMENT (-) WITHDRAWAL	√ T	FEE (-) IF ANY	(+) AMOUNT OF DEPOSIT	BALANCE
							75.00
	7/1	Deposit				225 00	225 00
							300 00
540	7/4	Dillard's	65 00				-65 00
		clothes					235 00
541	7/10	Allstate Insurance	126 59				-126 59
		car ins.					108 41
542	7/12	Wal-Mart	37 25				-37 25
		supplies					71 16
	7/15	Deposit				225 00	225 00
							296 16
543	7/15	Cash	20 00				-20 00
		movies					276 16
544	7/15	Blockbuster	34 65				-34 65
		CD's					241 51

BE SURE TO DEDUCT ANY PER ITEM CHARGES, SERVICE CHARGES, OR AUTOMATIC TELLER TRANSACTIONS WHEN APPLICABLE, ADD INTEREST EARNED. BE SURE TO RECORD ALL PREAUTHORIZED PAYMENTS/DEPOSITS ON DATE SCHEDULED.

NUMBER	DATE	TRANSACTION DESCRIPTION	PAYMENT (-) WITHDRAWAL	√T	(-) FEE IF ANY	(+) AMOUNT OF DEPOSIT	BALANCE
							241.51
545	7/15	Quick Stop	16 00				-16 00
		gas					225 51
ATM	7/15	Deposit				20 00	20 00
		check/Cindy					245 51
ATM	7/21	Withdrawal	22 00		.5		-22 50
							223 01

BE SURE TO DEDUCT ANY PER ITEM CHARGES, SERVICE CHARGES, OR AUTOMATIC TELLER TRANSACTIONS. WHEN APPLICABLE, ADD INTEREST EARNED. BE SURE TO RECORD ALL PREAUTHORIZED PAYMENTS/DEPOSITS ON DATE SCHEDULED.

back of the statement, there will be a place for listing these checks and the total. You have now identified your *Outstanding Checks*. Remember that term?

Step Two—Deposits in Transit

You may not have any of these gems, but at least find out for sure. Look in your checkbook and see if all recent deposits that you have made to your account are listed on your statement. If not, the total of these will be *Deposits in Transit*. Write this figure down or enter it on the form.

Step Three—Reconciling Items

Now look for any "reconciling items." Your service charge, if any, will be one of these. There may be a charge for printed checks if you recently ordered some. Items such as those just mentioned should be subtracted from the balance in your checkbook. If you were paid interest, add that positive reconciling item. If you are using the form, there is a place for this total. If not, just write down the total, making sure you have the value (positive or negative) correct. Make sure you enter in your checkbook any charges against your account and any interest that was paid to your account.

Step Four—Balancing Your Checkbook

The first three steps were preparation. Now comes the simple math. Take the ENDING BALANCE, subtract your OUTSTANDING CHECKS, add any DEPOSITS IN TRANSIT, add and/or subtract any RECONCILING ITEMS (usually subtract), and the result should equal the balance shown in your checkbook. Now, wasn't that easy? Amazing! One, two, three, four!

Okay, so something went wrong, and you're out of whack. Don't get discouraged or lose faith. This is exactly why you balance your checkbook to begin with. If you have made an error in your records, you want to know about it. This gives you a chance to find and correct it before you unknowingly write an NSF check.

Let's get started on finding that error. There are some logical things to look for. First, of course, recheck your math. Go back over your figures, and be careful not to make the same mistake twice. If that didn't do it, the next thing to do is to recheck the total of the outstanding checks you are subtracting from the ending statement balance (Step One). Next, bite the bullet and recheck all the math in your checkbook since the last time you proved your balance was right. This is a source of common mistakes that don't get corrected until you balance your checkbook each month.

Don't be discouraged if you don't balance on the first try

If you still have not found the error, you need to start checking some detail. Take each paid check that came with the bank statement and compare it with the amount you entered in your book when you wrote each check. You could have transposed two digits, such as writing the check for $11.43 but entering it as $11.34.

If you are still messed up, look for what is called an "encoding error." This is a step that occurs at a bank. A real live human reads the amount of the check and causes a machine to print an "encoded" amount on the bottom right of the face of the check. The machine prints this encoded amount with magnetic ink. This way other machines can read the numbers. It doesn't happen often, but mistakes can be made in encoding checks.

If you find a mistake, call the institution. Give someone the information on the check. Your bank has a picture of it, and a bank employee can see if a mistake was made. Someone will then enter a correction, or adjustment, on your account. That adjustment will show up on your next statement. Ask the banker to send you a memo so you don't have to wait for your next statement to be sure that the correction was made. Do not adjust your checkbook. The bank is telling you that a correction is being made. You automatically should be in balance next month without doing anything. Of course, all this assumes that the amount of the mistake agrees with the amount of the error you discovered. If so, all is okay. But it is not uncommon for there to be multiple errors (usually yours) in one statement. So keep looking until you find every mistake.

There are still one or two rare curve balls that might come your way. It is possible, but unlikely, that once or twice in your life someone else's check could get paid against your account. Also, your deposit could get posted to someone else's account. These occasions are rare, but they represent more reasons to reconcile your account each month.

Now you know all about handling your checking account. You now know a lot more than do people who go through life frequently messing up their accounts.

Electronic technology makes it very easy to keep your checkbook and to reconcile your account. Chuck Taylor uses his computer and the Quicken program to do the task.

ATM (Automated Teller Machine)

Another example of how technology is making our lives easier is the ATM. These machines are valuable and convenient tools. They are also cheaper for an institution to operate than a regular branch office. There is no other way a commercial bank, credit union, or savings and loan could give you access to your money all night and all over the world.

These machines, and the use of them, have really caught on with consumers. To give you some idea of how popular they are, today there are over 200,000 of them in the United States alone. And, the number of ATMs has been growing at about 15 percent per year.

ATMs give you access to your money
all night and all over the world

But, ATMs must be treated with a great deal of respect, like any other powerful tool. Like many people do, you can use an ATM because of the convenience. You can easily get cash from your checking account. But, beware, a lot of people have messed up their checking account by using an ATM and failing to enter the transaction in their checkbook right then and later forgetting about it. Later, they get a notice that an NSF check has hit the bank, and they can't figure out why.

To use an ATM, you must first open a checking or savings account with a financial institution. You then are issued an ATM card, which is magnetically encoded with data that can be read electronically when the card is inserted into an ATM. When your account is opened, a computer randomly assigns you a PIN (Personal Identification Number). This is a secret number, and you need to guard it carefully. You may rest assured that no one at the bank knows what it is.

When you insert your card into the ATM, the machine "reads" the magnetic stripe and knows who you are. The ATM video screen asks you for your PIN. If you correctly enter your PIN, you have access to your accounts. You may inquire about any account you have with the institution, withdraw money from your checking or savings account, or even transfer money from one account to another.

Recent technology has provided other means of security in addition to the PIN number. For example, a scanner on the ATM may read your iris—that is, the pattern of the part of your eye surrounding the black pupil. Other systems use your voiceprint, or the sound patterns of your voice. When you open an account, these items are recorded in the computer's database. Then, when you use an ATM, your iris print or your voiceprint is matched against the one stored in the computer. If there is a match, the ATM knows that you are you! So, you can get your money.

The convenience of ATMs does raise a security issue. Because banks care very much about your safety, many publish safety tips for their customers. Because this is so important, we have published common tips below.

- Treat your ATM card like cash, checks, and credit cards. Protect it. If it's lost or stolen, report it to the financial institution immediately.

- Memorize your PIN (personal identification number). Don't write it on your card or store it in your wallet. Don't give it out on the phone. Don't tell it to anyone—not even family, friends, or bank employees.

- Check out the area before using an ATM. If it is poorly lit, or if you see someone suspicious, use another ATM. Report any lighting or safety problem to the institution. If you suspect or witness unusual activity, contact the police immediately.

- Be courteous when waiting to use an ATM. Give the person using it the same privacy you expect.

- Try not to use an ATM alone at night.

- Minimize the time you spend at an ATM. Have your card ready. Have any required forms filled out beforehand.

- Stand between the ATM and those waiting behind you in order to block their view of your transactions—especially when you enter your pin number.

- If you feel uncomfortable during an ATM transaction, hit the CANCEL key to stop the transaction and get your card back. Leave the area immediately.

- As soon as you've completed your ATM transaction, take your card, money, and receipt, and move away from the teller machine. Put your cash in your wallet or purse right away. Don't count it or expose it so that others can see it.

- Don't forget to take your receipt. You'll need it to verify the transaction against your monthly account statement.

- If someone demands money from you at the ATM, do not resist. Carefully note the description of the person(s), and call the police as soon as you can.

- If someone appears to be following you after you've left the ATM, drive to the nearest well-lit, well-populated area. Don't drive straight home.

- Stay alert while using the ATM. Be aware of your surroundings as you approach or leave the area. Stay visible while at the ATM and while moving to or from your car.

- Keep your engine running when using a drive-up ATM, so you can leave the area quickly.

If you are using a night depository, some of the same cautions will apply.

Charges for using an ATM can vary widely. You must find out about the fees your institution charges. If you use an ATM frequently, you can rack up big charges. Take responsibility, and make sure that you get the most for your money.

Debit Cards

Debit cards were much slower than credit cards to catch on with consumers, but are now rapidly gaining popularity. Basically the debit card allows you to "write a check" without writing a check. Present your debit card when making a purchase and, assuming you have enough money in your checking account, the deal is done. The amount of the purchase immediately is subtracted from your account balance and added to the merchant's bank account. It's all done electronically, and with the same system used for credit card purchases. You don't have to worry about the hassles of writing a check, and the merchant doesn't have to take the risk of accepting a bad check.

When using a debit card, you must be sure to enter immediately the transaction in your checkbook or register. Otherwise, you will forget.

Banking by Phone

Many, if not most, banks today offer automated telephone service. You can telephone in 24 hours a day and perform all sorts of functions. With most institutions you can inquire about your current balance, get the details of your last transactions, find out how much interest you've earned, see if a check has cleared, transfer funds between accounts, issue a Stop Payment Request, reorder printed checks, and often many other functions. With most systems, when the bank is closed, you can even leave a message for someone to call you back! In most cases, the institution allows a very generous number of these services free each month. By combining modern technology with telephones, these fast and user-friendly systems can save you a time.

Banking on the Internet

An increasing number of banks enable you to conduct your banking business on the Internet. In fact, some banks have no brick-and-mortar branches and offer only Internet banking. You can click on the home page to open accounts, apply for loans, and secure other services.

Electronic payments systems permit you to transfer funds to others, avoiding paper checks entirely. Because the cost of doing business electronically is falling rapidly, no doubt more and more of our banking activities will involve the Internet. Banks enjoy the economics, and bank customers appreciate lower costs.

THINGS TO REMEMBER

A checking account is a powerful tool for managing money. It provides protection as well as convenience.

There are many kinds of checking accounts. When you open a checking account, learn about the choices and make the right one for you.

There is a time to use cash and a time to write checks. Don't be one of the people who flood the system with checks for just two or three dollars.

Writing a check without money in your account can lead to serious credit and legal problems. If you ever do make an honest mistake and write an NSF check, take care of it immediately.

A bank statement is a monthly summary of activity the bank has posted to your account. It may not always match the entries in your checkbook.

Balancing your checkbook each month with your bank statement will enable you to avoid unnecessary problems.

ATM machines offer a quick and convenient way to get money from your account and to conduct other banking business. But, as with any tool, you must learn to use ATMs properly.

A PIN must be kept secret.

Using a Debit Card is like writing a check electronically.

Part III

The Basics of Insurance and Taxes

Chapter Twelve

Car Insurance

Chuck Taylor was on his way home from work one evening. It was just seven months after he bought his neat car. As he was passing through an intersection, some guy in a pickup truck ran a red light. There was a collision. Even though Chuck wasn't to blame, the right front fender and door of his car were smashed. Talk about a sick feeling! Chuck almost couldn't look at the damage. He was thankful, however, that he wasn't hurt in the accident.

Damage to Chuck's car amounted to over $3,100. He had used nearly all of his savings for the down payment when he bought his car. How would he pay the repair bill? Fortunately, both Chuck and the driver of the pickup had "full" coverage insurance. Chuck was well covered from the financial damage of the wreck.

Here is another story—it really happened. For most of a year, a granddaughter of one of the authors had been saving money for an automobile. She had been working part-time at J. C. Penny while in high school, depending upon parents and friends for transportation. Getting to and from school and work was a real problem. She had been a very responsible daughter and got her driver's license at age 16. Her parents agreed that she would be allowed to buy a car if she wanted it bad enough to save up the necessary money.

She saved rapidly because she was able to work a lot of hours and maintain her grades. She recently bought a real clean six-year old Toyota hatchback for $2,500. She had not quite saved the full amount of the purchase price plus sales tax. But it was an exceptional buy, so her parents loaned her the $500 necessary to complete the deal. Of course, the law, and her parents, required that she buy liability insurance at least.

She decided to purchase just liability insurance. Collision and comprehensive would have cost another $180 every six months; so, she chose not to purchase the "extra" coverage. After all, she wasn't planning to need it! On the thirteenth day of owning the car, she ran a red light and hit another auto. Her pride and joy was destroyed. Not just damaged, but "totaled." Fortunately, there were no serious injuries. Her liability insurance covered the damage she did to the other driver's car, but she was up the proverbial creek. No money, no car, and she owed her parents $500.

The moral of this story is why we even have such a thing as insurance to begin with. Insure what you cannot afford to lose. There is a solid case for not insuring a six-year-old $2,500 automobile, but only if you can afford the loss if you wreck it. If you can't afford the loss and can't afford the cost of insuring what you can't afford to lose, then you have no business being in the game in the first place.

Protecting you and your car isn't "kid stuff"

Read on to find out what "full" coverage means. Find out how Chuck was well covered financially, and why he was not in the same financial bind as the fine young lady.

Find out the difference between "liability" and "collision" insurance, and many other critical facts that you need to know about car insurance.

Life is full of risk, as both Chuck and the granddaughter found out. Some risks we are stuck with. Other risks can be transferred to someone else. For a price, we can shift some of our risks to insurance companies. So you need to know about insurance.

If you are ever going to own anything, you must know how to protect your property. On top of that, and maybe even more important, you have a responsibility to protect the rest of the world from any damage *you* may cause.

The big world of insurance can be very complicated. We stay with the basics here to keep things simple. If you don't learn the basics about the kinds of insurance you may need, sooner or later you may pay a very heavy price.

We do not cover everything about insurance. However, if you learn what's here, you will be off to a good start, and you will probably know more than a lot of people.

In 1898, there were about 100 cars on the road in the entire nation. That's a little hard for us to visualize, but it's true. Nobody worried much about two cars being in a wreck with each other. There were dangers nonetheless. The biggest risk was that a noisy car would scare a horse! While a few people had cars, the rest of the world was riding around in horse and buggies. Horses often would panic when one of the loud contraptions came down the street. Frightened horses then would stampede in terror, dragging the buggy and its hapless occupants along with it. This kind of happening brought about the need for automobile insurance. The first policy was sold in the United States in 1898.

Things have changed. Now there are more than 200 million cars on the road. That number, of course, includes Chuck's new car!

One thing is certain. The automobile is the greatest danger to your life and to your pocketbook that you are ever likely to encounter. In a matter of seconds, a trip to get a hamburger can cost your life or someone else's life. Without adequate insurance, a moment of innocent carelessness can destroy you financially. Since all of us drive or ride in cars, we had better be glad there are insurance companies, even if we hate paying the premiums they charge.

For Chuck, buying the car was exciting and fun. But owning an auto is serious business. You see, having a car exposes you to a lot of risk. Not only is a car a fairly valuable asset, but it can be a source of harm to the owner and others in case of an accident. Fortunately, Chuck passed on most of that risk to an insurance company.

The Different Kinds of Car Insurance

Here is where the confusion starts for most people. We have to know what kinds of car insurance coverage there are and what kind we need. There are many parts of insurance that go into the policy we buy. Each part insures us against different things.

Liability Insurance

We start with the most important kind of car insurance. Liability insurance pays for injuries or damage that you may cause. The entire concept of liability is based on laws that say we each are responsible for our own actions. If we injure another person or cause damage to his or her property, we must compensate that person. But how many of us can pay for thousands of dollars in property damage, or millions for loss of life? That's why we pay premiums to insurance companies. By doing so, we transfer the risk to the insurance company.

When you buy liability coverage as part of an auto insurance policy, you protect yourself—to the limits of the policy—in several ways. In return for your premium dollars, the insurance company agrees to stand good for you for accidental damage caused if:

- You are driving a vehicle named in the policy.

- You are driving someone else's car with his or her permission.

- Someone is driving your car with your permission.

Liability insurance also provides another very critical form of protection for you. The insurance company agrees to defend you in a lawsuit resulting from an accident someone claims you caused. This is only one more of many reasons you must never be without liability insurance.

Your liability insurance covers only damage you cause to other people or their property. It does not cover you or your car.

Limits of Liability

When you buy liability coverage as part of an automobile insurance policy, you must select "limits" of coverage. Most policies have what are called "split-limits." These are expressed as "10/20/10" or "50/100/25." The numbers refer to thousands of dollars.

- The first figure is the limit the insurance company will pay for injuries per person in each accident;

- The second is the maximum total that will be paid for the injuries of two or more people for each accident; and

- The last figure applies to property damage.

In other words, if one person is hurt, the first figure is the most that the insurance company would pay. If more than one person is hurt in the same accident, the second figure is the limit of your insurance. So, if 10 people are hurt, that amount must cover all 10 injuries.

The laws of most states require each owner of a car to have a certain minimum amount of liability coverage, say 10/20/10. That's really not much coverage. If you cause $100,000 in injuries and you bought a low-limit policy, you are responsible for everything above the limits of the policy.

The amount of coverage you select affects your premium. Normally you can choose higher coverage for only a few dollars more than lower coverage would cost. We strongly recommend that you purchase more than the minimum amount the law requires. You should protect yourself with higher coverage.

Uninsured Motorists Insurance

This part of an auto policy is often misunderstood. Under most terms and conditions, this part of a policy does not fix your car in case of an accident if the other driver doesn't have insurance. But, it will cover injuries to you and your passengers caused by either another driver who does not have insurance or by a hit-and-run driver. As with all forms of insurance, you choose the limits of coverage. Uninsured motorists coverage is a low-cost option in most policies. It usually makes good sense to add this when you buy a policy.

Medical Payments Coverage

This one is pretty much what it says. If you choose this in your policy, you and anyone in your car are covered up to the set limits stated in the policy. This coverage pays for medical treatment of injuries resulting from the accident. It does not matter whose fault the accident is. This one even covers you if you are hit by a car while walking.

Collision and Comprehensive

Now we come to the kind of insurance that pays for damage to or the loss of your car. If you finance your car, the lender will usually require you to purchase this kind of insurance. Just about every auto financing contract in the world requires you to keep the car covered with collision and comprehensive insurance until the loan is paid. Chuck's bank required him to have this coverage on the car that was financed for him. Lenders want to know that their collateral will be protected. You do not have to purchase insurance through the lender. You may purchase the coverage from someone other than the lender. That often, if not always, will be cheaper.

Collision Insurance

This is the insurance that pays to fix your car if you have a wreck, whether it's your fault or not. There is no specified limit in the policy. Most policies will not pay for repairs that cost more than your car is worth. If the repairs exceed the value of the car, it is considered to be "totaled." An insurance company will not buy you a new car! Rather, the insurance company will pay you the value of the car at the time of the accident. If the car is financed, the check probably will be payable jointly to you and to the lender. You will have to settle up with the lender.

Remember in another chapter we warned about the dangers of financing an automobile for too long a term? Here is another example of that trap if you went for the low, low payments. You may owe $10,000 on a car that really is only worth $7,000 on the market. That doesn't hit you in the face if you are content to drive the car for a long time. But, were you to total the car in a wreck, the insurance company would only pay you $7,000. So, you still owe the creditor $3,000 and you are on foot! That is something to think about.

Collision insurance always has "deductibles." This means you are responsible for the damage up to the amount of the deductible you have chosen. The insurance kicks in for the loss in excess of the deductible. The lower the deductible, the higher the premium, and vice-versa. Deductibles you can choose typically range from $100 to $1,000.

Again, no matter who is at fault, the insurance company will pay. However, if the other driver is at fault, he or she owes you for your deductible—if you can collect it.

You should always call your insurance agent or company and let someone there know if you have been in an accident. If the other driver is at fault and has insurance, you should file a claim against the other driver's insurance company. After all, you don't want your insurance to pay unless you can't collect from the other driver.

Your collision insurance will pay for your damages even if the other driver does not have insurance. Later, the insurance company will try to collect from the other driver. The company has that right. For the record, this is called "subrogation."

Comprehensive Insurance

This is the coverage that pays for things other than an accident. This coverage protects your investment if your car is stolen or damaged by vandalism, if your windshield is broken, or even if your car catches fire and burns. Comprehensive coverage usually is very broad. Here, too, the amount of the premium you pay for this coverage is affected by the deductible you choose.

Do You Need Collision and Comprehensive?

If your car is financed, that decision will be made by whoever granted you the credit to buy the car. If your car is paid for, then you have the choice. You have to weigh the cost of the insurance against the value of your car. You must consider your ability to pay for repairs yourself, or to replace the car if it is totaled. If the car is valuable and you don't have a lot of savings, then you better spring for the insurance. If it's a "rag" and you can afford to buy another one if it burns, maybe you would be better off taking a chance that you won't have a wreck. Put the premiums in the bank, and you may be ahead.

The general rule about this kind of decision is to take a chance only with what you are willing and able to lose.

What to Do if You Have an Accident

First and foremost, do not admit any liability or fault. At the time of an accident, you may be upset and confused about the wreck. You really may not know if you are at fault or not. Don't jump out of the car yelling or accusing the other driver, either. The scene of an accident is not the place to get into an argument with the other driver.

The police should be called immediately. If there are injuries, tell the police that on the telephone. Assuming no one is hurt, wait for the police. You may want to exchange information, such as insurance policy information, with the other driver. Don't move your car until the police arrive and tell you to. Don't worry about who is at fault. Just tell the police officers the facts when they get there.

Afterwards, you should notify your insurance agent or company. Notifying the company is not the same as filing a claim. Even if the wreck is not your fault and the other driver has insurance, you should notify your insurance company. If you have trouble collecting from the other party, you can contact your insurance company again for help or to file a claim on your policy if that becomes necessary.

Discounts on Your Insurance

Most companies offer many kinds of discounts. If you have picked a good agent, he or she will help you save the most money possible on your policy. Knowing these tips will help you get the most for your money.

- Good Driver Discount—This is a discount for having a clean record. It means you've received no tickets for moving violations and no wrecks have been charged to you for the last three to five years.

- Economy Car Discount—Smaller cars cause less damage in an accident and are cheaper to repair. Therefore, they cost less to insure.

- Good Student Discount—These are for the bright (or hard-working) students who get good grades, usually a "B" average or better.

- Drivers Education Discount—Most companies will give a discount for anyone who has completed or who is taking a Drivers Education course. These are taught in most high schools. Drivers Ed can also be taken by any driver at a commercial school.

- Multi-Auto Discount—Most companies will give a discount if you own and insure two or more cars with the same company. Sometimes, depending on the company and on how the cars are licensed, one car can be a student's and the other can be Dad's. They both must be in the same household and located at the same place.

- Low Mileage Discount—If you don't drive a lot of miles in a year, you may be able to get a discount.

Ask your insurance agent or company about any other discount that may be available.

What Is an "Assigned Risk"?

This is what happens to you if you don't qualify for regular insurance. You go into a "pool." Your application for insurance is assigned to a company on a rotating basis. Each insurance company is obligated to accept "assigned risk" applications based on a complicated formula governed by the state. These policies carry much higher premiums.

You get put into a pool when you have too many wrecks or get too many traffic tickets. A conviction for driving under the influence of alcohol is guaranteed to get you thrown into the pool. Generally, anyone in the "assigned risk" program can get out and qualify for regular rates again after maintaining a good record for a certain number of years.

Keep your record clean, because you don't want to have to pay high premiums. You don't want to be an "assigned risk."

A Word of Caution

You wouldn't lend thousands of dollars to people whom you really don't know well, or couldn't prove were good risks, would you? Just because they smile at you and promise that they will repay you is not enough. You would check them out, just like any lender would before making a loan. You want to know about their ability to repay you and about their reputation.

Yet, people often buy auto insurance without first checking the reputation and financial condition of the insurance company. When you buy any type of insurance policy, you pay money to the company in exchange for a promise that the company will pay you if it becomes required under the terms of the policy. It's much like a loan transaction. You are actually extending credit (your trust) to them! So you'd better be careful about selecting an insurance company.

There are some fly-by-night outfits around. In a number of states, including Louisiana and Alabama, some big operations have gone "belly-up" in recent years. They took in a lot of premium dollars, but that money seems to have disappeared. When claims started piling up, the policyholders didn't get paid! Those companies have been shut down, but thousands of people may never get their money. In only the two states we mentioned, one company alone failed to pay out millions of dollars in valid claims that were owed to people.

Let the buyer beware! You should check out any insurance company before you sign a policy contract or make a payment. Policyholders may avoid a loss simply by calling their state insurance commission and requesting a report on their insurance company. Better Business Bureaus, too, often have files on insurance companies who fail to pay claims satisfactorily. Do business only with reputable agents and companies—ones that have a proven and solid track record.

THINGS TO REMEMBER

Liability Insurance protects you from the claims of others you may injure or whose property you may damage. Each of us is responsible for damage we cause to the property of others or for injury to people. Liability insurance does not pay for damages to your car.

Make sure your limits of liability are adequate. Higher limits cost very little more than low ones.

Uninsured Motorists Insurance normally covers only injury to you or your passengers if the other party in an accident does not have insurance. It does not cover your car.

Comprehensive and Collision Insurance protects *your* property, no matter who is at fault. You will be protected even if the other driver in an accident does not have insurance. This insurance does not cover your responsibility to anyone else if you have an accident.

If your car is an older one with little value, you should consider not carrying collision.

If you have an accident, do not admit liability, and do not be unpleasant or get into an argument. Call the police immediately.

There are often discounts on car insurance.

Assigned Risk is a pool of insurance for people who do not qualify under normal conditions. It is expensive.

Carefully check out insurance companies before you sign up or pay. Be sure the one you select is reputable and financially sound.

Chapter Thirteen

Other Kinds of Insurance

Chuck Taylor is relatively young. He's not married, and besides his car loan, he doesn't owe much money. He has protected his automobile investment with collision and comprehensive insurance. In addition, he has protected himself with liability coverage. Sales people contact him frequently trying to sell him other insurance. They will be calling you, too, before long, if they haven't already. You need to have a grip on the basics of life insurance and other kinds of insurance.

Life Insurance

In one form or another, life insurance has been around for a long time. Today, more than $5 trillion worth of life insurance is in force in the United States. That's a 5 with 12 zeros on the end!

There are different kinds of life insurance policies. We limit this discussion to the two most common—whole life and term life. Life insurance pays money to the named beneficiary when the insured person dies. The basic purpose of life insurance is to provide for the financial security of family members who depended on the income of the insured person during his or her life.

Life insurance provides for the financial security of those people who depend on your income

Whole Life

If someone dies during the period of coverage, the insurance company pays the face value of a policy to the beneficiary. If premiums are paid long enough, then "cash value" will build up and will be paid if the policy is "cashed in," even before death. The insured person can even borrow this cash value. It can also be used to pay premiums to keep the insurance in force when income is lost or reduced.

Remember one basic fact. A whole life policy, no matter what it is called, is an investment product combined with insurance protection. Whole life insurance is much more expensive than term insurance, which we explain a little later. There is nothing wrong with your choosing this kind of combination investment and insurance, but you should take the time to understand the choices and the costs of this kind of insurance policy.

There are many "spin offs" of this basic kind of policy. They are known by a lot of names. Many of them are very similar. All are designed to compete for and attract your insurance dollar. The facts you have learned about our free enterprise market economy apply here also. We have a lot of choices to make—and we have the responsibility to ourselves to learn how to make them.

Term Insurance

This is the simplest and cheapest of all life insurance policies. For a given premium and for as long as you pay it according to terms, you get a certain amount of life insurance. If you die while the policy is in force, your beneficiary gets paid. If you cancel the policy or stop paying the premiums, you or your beneficiary get nothing. With term insurance, you pay a low price specifically to provide some money for a loved one if you die. Term insurance comes in many forms, but the concept is the same for each form. Many employers offer term insurance as an employee benefit.

Premiums for all life insurance policies are governed by the type of policy, your age, your health, and sometimes even your occupation. As you get older, your annual premium increases. Often there is a discount if you don't smoke, because evidence shows that non-smokers live longer. Also, premiums for women may be cheaper than for men. Data show that women live longer. If you have certain kinds of dangerous hobbies, insurance premiums could be higher.

A note here about beneficiaries. Our lives change, often in many ways. As only one example, a young, single person may obtain some form of life insurance and make his or her parents the beneficiary. Later, he or she gets married, but forgets that the parents are still beneficiary. You should always remember to change your insurance beneficiary as necessary. That way the person you wish will get the money, should something happen to you.

There are many, many more details about life insurance, but now you know the most important facts. Find a trustworthy, knowledgeable agent to help you. But remember that the agent gets a commission on all the insurance that he or she can sell you.

Medical or Health Insurance

When Chuck was a little younger, he thought he was invincible. He never thought about getting sick or having a serious injury. Chuck didn't think much about health insurance. When he got a good job that had health benefits provided for him, he still didn't think much about it. But a young friend at work was seriously injured in a car wreck. He was in the hospital nearly two weeks. When he was back at work, he told Chuck that, without insurance, he would have been ruined financially. Chuck began to realize that if it could happen to a friend, it could happen to him.

*Lack of health insurance can cause
serious financial problems*

Medical or health insurance pays all or part of doctor bills and hospital charges if you get sick or are injured in an accident. In some policies, other miscellaneous medical expenses, such as ambulance service, are covered as well. Some policies may even cover part of the costs of treatment for mental health. The cost of health care in recent years has soared, and without good health insurance, an illness or accident could wipe you out financially.

The need for public access to affordable health care is of great national concern. Many people do not have any medical insurance. They are often unable to pay for needed treatment. This tends to overburden charity health systems, funded by our tax dollars. There is a strong push by some to create some form of socialized medicine. But, that approach has not worked well in other countries. As with many problems, there are no easy solutions, only difficult choices.

Health insurance may cover part or all of necessary expenses for treatment of four main areas: hospitalization, surgery, doctor visits, and major medical expenses resulting from long or severe illness or injury. Most policies will have deductibles and co-insurance requirements. A deductible is an amount you must pay before the insurance takes over. Co-insurance means that the insurance company pays a percentage (usually 80%) of costs, and you pay the remaining percentage. Many, if not most, health insurance policies have what is called a "stop loss" provision. That says that once you pay out a certain amount, the insurance then pays 100% up to the limits of the policy.

Chuck, however, belongs to an HMO (Health Maintenance Organization) through his employer, as a part of his job benefits. HMOs usually are not insurance companies. HMOs are organizations made up of enrolled doctors, hospitals, and other health care providers. Chuck pays only $20 each time he needs medical care, whether it is a doctor visit, emergency treatment, or hospitalization. He must normally, however, go to a doctor or provider who is a member of that HMO. This kind of health care program can be excellent, but is often expensive. A set monthly amount is paid to the HMO, much the same as if it were an insurance premium. Chuck got a job with excellent benefits, and his employer pays most of this monthly amount. He is very lucky because most part-time workers do not get such benefits. His employer clearly wants to hire Chuck full-time when he graduates from college.

Most medical and health insurance is provided through group policies. Employers arrange this coverage with insurance companies and provide some or all of the premium cost as a benefit to the employee. Self-employed people, or those who work at a business that does not provide medical insurance, must purchase an individual policy if they wish coverage.

Under many circumstances, insurance companies will require that you take a medical examination before they will provide you coverage. This is true not only for health insurance, but often for life insurance also. If the tests indicate that you have AIDS or that you use illegal drugs, it is almost impossible for you to get a policy. In the case of group policies arranged by employers, there may be a provision for enrollment without a physical.

Health and Accident Insurance

This insurance, usually called H&A, is very limited in coverage and benefits. It must not be confused with true health insurance described in previous examples. The policies are often low-cost, but pay limited amounts only for specified occurrences. They will rarely even begin to cover the full cost of treatment. They may, for example, pay you $75 per day if you are hospitalized for a covered event. This won't go far. Hospital stays can easily exceed $1,000 or more per day. Health and accident insurance is aggressively promoted by mail. Frequently, you will receive mail urging you to buy this insurance.

Residential or Property Insurance

This kind of insurance offers protection to people who own their homes. It also can be bought by someone renting an apartment or a home. In the first case, the insurance includes protection for personal property and the value of the home. In the second case, it covers the tenant's (renter's) personal property. Both types usually include liability insurance or personal protection. This very important protection will cover you if your dog bites somebody, or if somebody falls and is injured while visiting you. This liability insurance is usually very broad in coverage and very important to have. This liability insurance does not cover your car. That must be separate.

We are not going into any more detail about this kind of insurance, because there are so many different coverages and options. When you first get an apartment, find a good insurance agent who will explain your choices. Just ask him or her questions. If the agent doesn't make you comfortable with the answers, find another agent.

When the time comes to buy your first home, the mortgage company will require you to have homeowners insurance to protect its mortgage.

Other Kinds of Insurance

There are other kinds of insurance, such as disability insurance, credit life insurance, and mortgage cancellation insurance (which is a type of credit life insurance). Unless you go to work in the insurance business, you will never learn about all kinds of policies! There are so many. As you go through life, learn how to ask questions and protect yourself. And do business only with reputable people and companies. If you put the information about insurance that we have provided to good use, you will make wiser decisions than many people are able to do.

Where to Get Insurance

Insurance is available from knowledgeable people known as agents, directly from insurance companies, and on the Internet from both agents and the companies. Agents often represent a number of insurance companies and are able to offer you personal service as well as their expertise. But that service and knowledge comes with a price. You can find cheaper insurance rates on the Internet. Check out the web sites offering life insurance and auto insurance. However, you need to make certain that the savings justify the loss of personalized service from a reputable agent.

THINGS TO REMEMBER

Life insurance is designed primarily to benefit your loved ones and family members who are dependent upon your income.

Term life policies offer insurance on your life at low premiums. Whole life insurance combines forms of investment with the insurance, but at a much higher premium.

Health insurance can be critically important and often can be arranged with group policies through employee benefit programs.

Health care costs in the United States are rising dramatically and are a national concern.

Property insurance can be purchased both by homeowners and renters to cover personal belongings from fire, theft, and other causes of loss.

Take the initiative to make sure an insurance company is reputable and financially sound. The time to do this is before you sign a contract or pay a premium.

Chapter Fourteen

You and the IRS

Chuck Taylor still remembers his very first payday during the summer that he first worked. He was excited, to put it mildly. He could hardly wait to get that fat paycheck in his hands. Chuck was making $5.15 an hour at the time, and he had been able to work 92 hours that two-week pay period. He had done his figuring and knew that check would be $504.70, counting the overtime pay. Chuck had plans for that money.

But what a shock! When he got his check, it was only for $405.09. His employer had held out $38.61 for FICA (Social Security tax and Medicare) and $61.00 for federal income tax. Had the bookkeeper made a mistake? No. Chuck simply had forgotten about deductions for federal income tax and Social Security tax. Chuck had heard of these things before, but really never associated them with himself until now. Chuck asked the bookkeeper about these deductions from his paycheck. The bookkeeper told Chuck that when he filled out his W-4, he had claimed zero dependents. Well, Chuck had thought since he wasn't married and had no children, he didn't have any dependents! That was a few years ago, and Chuck has learned a lot about taxes since then. You will also learn these things as you read this chapter.

Laws require that, in nearly all cases, an employer take out these taxes. This is called "withholding." Most workers have to pay federal income taxes and, in many states, state income taxes also. Later in this chapter you will learn more about when and how much.

Our tax laws are so complicated that even the experts often are confused. But, fear not! In this book we cover only the bare bones about taxes. These are important facts. Nobody wants to get into trouble with Uncle Sam. But, tens of thousands of people do because they never learned a few simple things. We're not talking about tax cheats, but about honest people who didn't know what they should have known.

We have said before in this book that a lot about life isn't fair, and that includes taxes. Most people feel they have to pay too much in taxes because the government wastes money. Maybe that's true, but we can't help you there. Take that up with your elected representatives! Don't forget that without taxes, we wouldn't even have roads or bridges, let alone the many valuable services government provides.

This chapter does not try to teach you how to save money on taxes. We stick to informing you about the tax system and telling you of certain responsibilities that you have.

Our Tax System

The subject of taxes is one that we all probably would like to ignore. But taxes are a reality of life, and we pay them to the local, state, and federal governments. The federal agency called the Internal Revenue Service (IRS) is the biggest and most important player in the game. The IRS collects taxes under laws passed by Congress. The federal taxes and particularly the tax on the income that we earn and otherwise receive takes the biggest bite out of our pocketbook. So, we focus mainly on income taxes in this chapter.

According to the Tax Foundation, about 100 years ago, federal, state, and local taxes combined amounted to about $20 per person. If you adjusted that for the increase in prices (called inflation) that has occurred since then, it would be equal to more than $340 per person at the present time. But, our individual tax burden has increased much faster than inflation. Are you ready for a shock? Now taxes at all levels of the government amount to $10,298 for every man, woman and child in the United States. In other words, your share is way over $10,000. Fortunately, someone else probably is paying that for you now. But soon, you'll be paying that much and maybe more all by yourself.

We pay taxes in the form of sales tax and property tax to local governments. If you don't own any property and just rent an apartment, you still are paying the property tax. You see, your landlord will add the tax into the amount of rent that you pay.

Some states put a tax on the income that you receive, others get a chunk of the property tax, and many get a sales tax along with other taxes such as taxes on gasoline. Most of the federal government money comes from income taxes, although a pretty good chunk of it comes from taxes on gasoline, cigarettes, telephone service, and other excise taxes.

How big is the total burden that people bear to cover spending by government at all three levels? According to the Tax Foundation, if the government withheld all of the money from every American's paycheck starting on the first day of the year, it would have to continue taking every bit of each American's paycheck until May to collect enough money to pay for local, state, and federal government activities.

A tax is somewhat like a fine. It is a penalty that you pay in the form of money. When we tax productive labor, we impose a penalty on it. And, whatever you penalize, you get less of. For example, if there were no fine for running stoplights, many people would just run the stoplights whenever they wanted. But, to avoid the fine, most people stop for stoplights. Of course, there are safety factors that enter into the decision to stop for a red light also! So it is with taxes. What you penalize, you get less of.

The federal government takes the tax money that it collects from wage earners and spends that money the way Congress decides. Much of the money is used to subsidize certain things and activities. It is a fact that whatever you subsidize, you get more of.

So, our elected politicians have got to balance the penalty factor of taxes along with the subsidy impact of government spending. In the meanwhile, they have got to please the voters.

Tax Withholding

Most of our income tax is withheld from workers' paychecks. In other words, on payday, each worker gets the income he or she earned less the money that is withheld to pay income tax and Social Security tax. In the example at the beginning of this chapter, Chuck ended up with less take-home pay than the amount he earned. That was because some of the money to pay his taxes was taken before he even got his hands on his paycheck.

By taking a little bit of your income out of each of your paychecks, the government gets to use the money quicker and it reduces the complaints from taxpayers. In other words, there is less of a negative impact when the taxes are taken a bit at a time rather than all at one time. Perhaps there would be considerable complaining about taxation and government spending if every taxpayer had to write a check out of his or her bank account each April 15 for the whole year's worth of income taxes!

Who Pays Income Taxes?

In the United States we have a progressive income tax system. That is, the more money you make, the higher the tax rate is. In other words, as your income increases, the greater the proportion of your income you will have to pay to the federal government.

According to IRS reports for the most recent year for which data is available (tax year 1997), taxpayers having adjusted gross income of more than $200,000 accounted for just 15 people out of every 1,000 people filing returns. That 1.5% of the people, however, paid over 38% of all taxes paid by individuals!

At the other end, 19.2% of the people had adjusted gross incomes of less than $15,000. Those people paid just over 1% of all individual income taxes. Of course, some people had no taxable income and, therefore, paid no federal income tax at all.

At the turn of the century, federal taxes per every man, woman, and child in the United States amounted to $6,277—which was up from $5,150 just ten years before. That is a 22% increase in just a decade.

Where Does the Money Go?

The table shows the major categories of spending by the federal government for fiscal years 1999 and 1979. You can see the shift that has taken place over that 20-year period. Expenditures on healthcare have more than doubled as a percentage of total government spending, while defense spending as a percentage of total spending has dropped by nearly one-half.

There are two broad categories of government spending—entitlements and discretionary. Entitlements are those expenditures that the federal government has to make because laws passed in prior years created such programs. Most are social programs to benefit different groups of people. Discretionary expenditures are those for which Congress can decide to increase or decrease spending each year. Examples include defense spending, education, agriculture, and transportation. Recently, entitlements accounted for about 75 cents of every dollar of federal spending. Thirty years ago entitlements were less than one-third of government spending. So, increasingly, our tax money is going to pay for programs that Congress previously created, usually in attempts to curry the favors of certain categories of voters who benefit directly from the entitlement programs.

In a civilized society, we have governments. Those governments are expected to provide services people cannot provide for themselves. Like it or not, every society has had to have armies to defend itself against enemies. All reasonable people agree that we need things such as roads, bridges, schools, libraries, disaster relief, national parks, and so on. Add to that list things we wish we didn't need, but do, such as a congress to make laws, courts to enforce and interpret those laws, and useful and effective social programs to help those unable to help themselves. It all adds up to the fact that government must have a stream of income with which to provide these things.

All we have tried to do so far in this chapter is to help rationalize why we have to pay taxes. We don't have to like paying them! Next, we give you some basic facts about the income tax laws that affect you. If you take the time to learn these basics, you and the IRS may get along better.

What Is a Tax Return?

A tax return is a form that each taxpayer fills out and sends to the IRS each year. It can be one of several forms, which we explain later. Each completed tax form contains income and other information that must be supplied to the government. In the U.S., taxpayers provide their own information on these forms. But the IRS also collects a variety of data to ensure that taxpayers cannot easily cheat. The IRS is able to check up on what taxpayers report on their forms.

The purpose of the tax return is to compute the amount of income tax that the taxpayer owes for the period covered by the return. Of course, most wage earners have already paid all or most of their income tax because of the withholdings out of their paychecks.

Who Must File an IRS Return?

If you are a U.S. citizen or a foreign citizen who lives in the U.S. *and* have income above a certain amount, you must file a return. For example, in 1999 the income levels above which individuals must file a return were as follows.

Single $7,050

Married and filing a separate return.................$2,750

Married and filing a joint return $12,700

Filing as "Head of Household" $9,100

These numbers are scheduled to rise each year in order to compensate for inflation, so remember to check for the proper figures for any year later than 1999.

When to File

The deadline for filing a tax return is April 15 for most individuals. If April 15 falls on a weekend or legal holiday, the return may be filed on the next business day. That return covers the income earned during the prior calendar year.

You can get an automatic extension of four months to file either Form 1040 or 1040A by filing a request on Form 4868. This extension must be filed by April 15. However, that does not mean that you can delay in paying any taxes you owe! Payment for any estimated taxes due must be paid when you file for the extension. If you don't pay on time, you must pay penalties and interest.

Where to File

Returns are mailed to the Internal Revenue Service Center serving the region where you live. A list of filing locations is provided in the instruction booklet for Forms 1040 and 1040A provided by the IRS. Increasingly, taxpayers are filing electronically over the Internet. In a recent year, about one out of every five returns were filed electronically.

What Form to Use

Most people use one of three forms: Forms 1040, 1040A, and 1040EZ.

Only single or married filing jointly taxpayers with no dependents, and under age 65, may use Form 1040EZ. It's the shortest and easiest to use, and accounts for 17% of all returns filed.

Form 1040A is a two-page form accompanied by a two-page Schedule 1. You may use 1040A if you do not itemize deductions and if your income consists only of wages, salaries, tips, taxable scholarships and fellowships, unemployment compensation, pensions, annuities, IRAs, Social Security, railroad retirement benefits, dividends, and interest. Also, your taxable income must be less than $50,000 under the law in effect in 1999.

Any taxpayer whose needs or circumstances are other than those above should file using Form 1040. It is a complicated, complex form that may include several additional schedules. It's a real pain to fill out. About 55 of every hundred taxpayers are stuck with the 1040 curse!

What Is Taxable Income?

Taxable income is "Adjusted Gross Income"(AGI) minus allowances for deductions and exemptions. Adjusted gross income is simply your total income from all sources, less special deductions such as alimony paid, IRA contributions, or reimbursed employee expenses. Deductions can include such things as local property taxes, charitable contributions, and, in some rare cases, medical expenses.

Child support is not deductible by the person who pays it. Nor is it taxable to the person receiving it. Alimony is deductible by the person who pays it, and it is taxable to the person who receives it if it is paid because of court rulings.

What Is a Standard Deduction?

All taxpayers are entitled to a "Standard Deduction," whether they itemize deductions or not. The amount depends upon whether you are married, single, or a "head of household." Standard deduction amounts for 1999 were as follows. (Remember, these, too, are scheduled to change each year.)

Single $4,300

Married and filing jointly* $7,200

Married filing separately $3,600

Filing as head of household $6,350

*If one spouse files separately, the other cannot itemize.

Standard as well as itemized deductions simply represent income that is not subject to income taxes.

What Is an "Exemption"?

The full name is "personal exemption" or "dependency exemption," whichever the case. This is an amount that you can deduct from your gross income, lowering your taxable income. The amount for 1999 was $2,750 for each eligible exemption. This amount is adjusted annually to reflect the inflation rate.

Exemptions, like deductions, represent income on which you do not have to pay taxes.

Who Is a Dependent?

A dependent is someone for whom you provide the majority of financial support, and for whom you may claim a dependency deduction from your taxable income. You probably don't have any dependents right now! But some day you will, so read on. There are five tests that must be met to determine if you may claim a person as a dependent on your tax return. They are as follows:

1. The person must have less than $2,750 gross income for the year; unless the dependent is your child and either is under the age of 19 or is a full-time student under the age of 24.

   If a child earned over $2,750 and meets the age or student rule, he or she may be claimed as a dependent on his or her parent's return only if he or she does not claim himself or herself as a dependent on his/her own tax return

   You may have to read the above a couple of times to figure it out, but this is an important rule. The effect can be to lower a parent's tax rate and raise the child's. However, the child's tax rates are usually much lower.

2. The taxpayer must have furnished over one-half of the dependent's financial support. This situation is usually encountered when a taxpayer is taking care of a parent or relative, and the person has income to provide part of his or her own support.

   In the case of children of divorced or separated parents, the general rule is that the custodial parent gets the deduction, unless stated otherwise in a child-support or separation agreement.

3. The person must fall within one of the following relationships:

   (a) Son or daughter, grandchild, great grandchild, step-child, or adopted child

    (b) Brother or sister

    (c) Brother or sister by the half blood

    (d) Stepbrother or stepsister

    (e) Mother or father, ancestor of either

    (f) Stepfather or stepmother

    (g) Nephew or niece

    (h) Aunt or uncle

    (i) Generally, an in-law

    (j) A person who is a live-in, as long as the relationship does not violate local law and as long as that person lived with you the entire year.

4. The dependent must not have filed a joint return with his or her spouse. We think this says that a "friend" whom you support cannot be claimed as a dependent on your return if he or she files a joint return with a legal husband or wife!

5. The dependent must be a citizen, national, or resident of the United States, Canada, or Mexico. There are a few other conditions relative to this rule if the person is not a citizen.

Who Is a "Head of Household"?

Married couples filing joint returns receive somewhat more favorable treatment on tax rates than single people. To help offset this, the IRS provides a "Head of Household" filing category, with lower tax rates than the usual "single" filer.

To qualify as Head of Household, a taxpayer must not be married at the close of the tax year or must have lived separately from his or her spouse during the last six months of the year. In addition, the taxpayer must maintain as his or her home a household that is the principal place where one or more of the following lived for at least half of the year:

1. A son or daughter, a grandchild, an adopted child, a stepchild, or a foster child. If one of these is a foster child or is married at the close of the tax year, he or she must meet other dependency tests.

2. Any other relative eligible to be claimed as a dependent, *except* those eligible to be claimed under a multiple support agreement.

3. You may be considered a head of household even if your father or mother may live separately from you provided that you pay more than one-half of the cost of keeping up their main home.

Who Must Have a Social Security Number?

Any dependent over one year old that you are eligible to claim on your return must have a Social Security number. That number must be entered on your tax return.

The government issues Social Security numbers. To work, you must have such a number. Your Social Security number is used in reporting and recording tax information, and the government also uses it for other purposes.

What Is the Difference Between "Tax Liability" and "Withholding"?

Every time you are paid, your employer withholds some federal tax from your paycheck. This withholding will almost never equal your tax "liability" for the year. The amount your employer withholds each payday is determined by the W-4 form you fill out when you start your job. Your actual tax liability (the total amount of tax you must pay for the year) is determined by the results of completing your tax return. In completing your return, you list all of your income and take your deductions. These calculations determine your taxable income. Your actual tax that you owe on this amount of your income is determined from tax tables that the IRS provides you.

There are many circumstances that can cause your withholdings for the year to be more or less than the amount you actually owe. If too much of your money was withheld from your earnings during the year, you can get a refund when you file your tax return. If not enough money was withheld from your earnings, you owe more taxes that must be paid when you file your tax return form. Remember that any refund you get really is some of your <u>own</u> money that is being returned to you.

What Is a "W-2"?

This is a form that your employer is required to complete for you and for every employee that it had during the year. You get three copies: one for your records, one to file with your federal tax return, and one to file with any state or local tax return that may be required. Your employer sends the original to the IRS so that it will know how much income you had. That way the tax officials will know to expect you to file a tax return. You should get a W-2 for each job that you held during a year. The amount of wages shown on W-2s and any other income must be included in your gross income on your tax return.

What Is a "1099"?

A W-2 is used for reporting income from normal wages. But there are other kinds of income you may receive, such as interest on your savings or dividends on your investments. That income may be reported on what is called a "1099." There are many versions of a 1099, and each is for a different kind of income. If you receive a 1099 for work that you have performed and no Social Security tax was withheld, you may be required to pay that Social Security tax along with your income tax.

You will receive a 1099 if you receive income from any other source that the law requires to be reported. That income must be declared on your tax return.

What Is a "W-4"?

This is really a simple form, but one that is often misunderstood. When you are hired in a regular job, the employer is required by law to withhold your income taxes from your paycheck as described earlier. The amount of tax the employer is required to withhold is determined by the W-4 that you fill out for your employer

A W-4 form has only a few blanks to fill out, and it has instructions on how to do it. The purpose of the form is to help you know how many "allowances" to claim and what your filing "status" (married, single, etc.) will be. An allowance is similar to an exemption, except that when your employer refers to tax tables, the status and number of allowances will tell him or her how much tax must be withheld from your pay. Your employer then sends your money that has been withheld to the federal government.

The more allowances you are entitled to claim, the less tax will be withheld from your pay. If you do not claim as many allowances as you are entitled to, too much tax will be taken out each payday. When you file your tax return, you will get a refund. In that case, you will have let the government use some of your money interest free during the year.

If you have income only from one source, completing a W-4 is really easy. The form asks you if you are married or single, your name, address, and Social Security number, and how many allowances you are claiming. You are asked simple questions that tell you the number of allowances. Normally, you get one allowance for each dependent.

If you are married and your spouse is working, or you have other income, or pay childcare expenses, allowances can change. But again, the instructions are fairly clear.

Completing a W-4 correctly can be very important. If too much tax is withheld, you can always get it back. If you claim too many allowances and not enough of your money is held out as taxes, you will owe more money when you file your return. Sometimes, there can be additional penalties plus interest if you owe too much tax at the end of the year.

Income Tax Rates

In the U.S. we have a progressive tax rate structure. That simply means that as your taxable income goes up above certain levels, you move into higher and higher tax rate brackets. In other words, you pay a bigger percentage of your income to the federal government as your income grows.

For taxable income received during 1999, the brackets and rates were as follows. (Remember, these brackets, and perhaps the rates, change each year—so the numbers below refer to 1999 only.)

For Single Taxpayers

If your taxable income is less than $25,750, the tax rate is 15 percent.

If your taxable income is between $25,750 and $62,450, the tax is $3,802.50 plus 28 percent of the amount over $25,750.

If your taxable income is between $62,450 and $130,250, the tax is $14,138.50 plus 31 percent of the amount over $62,450.

If your taxable income is between $130,250 and $283,150, the tax is $35,156.50 plus 36 percent of the amount over $130,250.

If your taxable income exceeds $283,150, the tax is $90,200.50 plus 39.6 percent of the amount over $283,150.

For Married Taxpayers Filing Jointly

If your taxable income is less than $43,050, the tax rate is 15 percent.

If your taxable income is between $43,050 and $104,050, the tax is $6,457.50 plus 28 percent of the amount over $43,050.

If your taxable income is between $104,050 and $158,550, the tax is $23,537.50 plus 31 percent on the amount over $104,050.

If your taxable income is between $158,550 and $283,150, the tax is $40,432.50 plus 36 percent on the amount over $283,150.

If your taxable income exceeds $283,150, the tax is $85,288.50 plus 39.6 percent on the amount over $283,150.

As you study the above taxable amounts and rates, two facts about the current tax laws become obvious. First, people earning a higher income pay a larger share of their taxable income to the federal government. Second, our wise people in Washington feel that married people should pay higher tax rates! This is referred to as the "marriage penalty." Many politicians have said they would get rid of this penalty, but it hasn't happened yet.

What Is a "Tax Credit"?

A tax credit is not the same as a deduction. A deduction is an amount you can deduct from your *taxable* income. You pay taxes on the rest. A tax credit is something you can actually subtract from the final amount of tax that you owe to the government. Think about this a little, and you will see the big difference.

What Is "Earned Income Credit (EIC)"?

This fearsome expression is fairly simple (although nothing is really simple about tax laws). If you qualify for an

Earned Income Credit, believe it or not, you can actually get something for nothing.

The EIC is a special tax credit for certain workers. It reduces the tax you owe, or may give you a refund even if you don't owe any tax. The credit for 1999 was as much as $347 if you didn't have a qualifying child and were at least 25 years old. If you had one qualifying child, the credit could have been as much as $2,271. If you had more than one qualifying child, it was as much as $3,816. If you had a qualifying child and could take the credit, you had to fill in and attach Schedule EIC to your return.

The EIC was *designed* to give people an incentive to work and keep them off the welfare rolls. However, like many federal programs, it has expanded greatly and is often used by some people to receive money from the government for little work. People who do pay income taxes, of course, provide that money!

Special Notes About Taxes

If your income (under 1999 law) was under $7,050 and you were single, you were not even required to file a tax return. However, if taxes were held out from your paychecks, you must file a return to get those taxes refunded to you. Otherwise, the IRS keeps your money.

If you file a 1040EZ or a 1040, all you have to do is enter your name and address, Social Security number, attach your W-2s, sign the return, and send it in. The IRS will figure everything else for you. If you have a refund coming, you will get it. If you owe more, you will get a bill.

Some young people and their parents can get in a jam over this. They don't communicate; so the young person claims himself or herself as a dependent, and so do Mom and/or Dad. This is a "no-no." The same person cannot be claimed on two returns. In fact, if someone else can claim you as a dependent, you cannot claim yourself as a dependent.

Each year thousands of taxpayers unnecessarily pay fees to a "tax service" when they could easily file their own return. In the case of a 1040EZ or a 1040A, the IRS will do the work for you free. The 1040EZ has only five lines to complete, but there are people who will not even look at it. They take it somewhere and pay a fee. We hope this book has taught you enough not to be one of these people.

Many people also pay a fee to get their refund immediately rather than waiting a few weeks to receive it from the IRS. They pay a very high fee, or interest rate, for this. It is generally a very poor and costly practice. Also, it is a sign that people have not learned how to make smart decisions. Watch out for advertisements or offers that promise "instant tax refunds." Make sure you get the facts before making a decision that costs you money for very little benefit. You may be much better off just waiting a few weeks for any refund that may be coming to you.

Chuck's taxes help pay for new roads and repairs

Chuck Taylor is never very happy when he has to pay his federal income taxes. Yet he realizes that the government provides some important things for him and for all people. That new car he is driving wouldn't go very far without streets and highways! So, he pays his taxes like every good citizen. But also like a good citizen, he is learning to pay attention to the people running for elected offices. He is learning that what politicians stand for and what they do will affect him. He is registered to vote, and does so. He makes a real effort to learn about candidates for office and cast an intelligent vote. He doesn't want his money that he pays in taxes to be wasted by poor management, bad laws, and wasteful programs. Chuck invites you to care about, and work for, good and honest government. That's your civic responsibility. You have a stake in how the government spends your money.

You are paying taxes in one form or another—even if you do not have a job earning a paycheck. At the very least, every time you make a purchase, you are paying sales taxes. If you have a job and are earning money, you are paying Social Security taxes. If your earnings are enough to have taxable income, you are also paying income tax. So, you should care what the government does with the money you give to it.

Some politicians often talk about reducing the size of the federal government so that it takes less of your money. All of the rhetoric about reducing taxes and the size of government sounds good. Wouldn't you and your parents like to pay less in taxes? There are, however, serious problems to accomplishing all of these good things. We have something called "entitlement programs" in America. In general, these are programs that take tax money and transfer it to certain groups of people, generally lower income people. The largest of these are Social Security, Medicare, and Medicaid, but there are many more such programs. These entitlement programs, combined with the interest payments on the national debt—the money the government has borrowed in the past so that it could spend more than it collected in taxes—eat up 75% of the federal budget. Defense spending is only 15.5%. This means everything else the government spends is only 12% of the budget. Now you can get an idea of how little is spent on roads and bridges!

It will be impossible to make meaningful inroads on reducing what the government spends without cutting entitlement programs.

If the politicians really attempt to cut entitlement programs, there will be a great amount of hollering and scream-
ing and crying "foul." It will be painful for the people who
have gotten used to the programs. It is not our purpose to
take sides on this issue, but to point out some facts to you.
All through this book we have attempted to help you understand that there is no such thing as a free lunch. As you
take your place in our economic system as a taxpayer, you
will have to decide for yourself how you feel about such
things.

Our system of taxation attempts to perform what is
known as "social engineering." In other words, the federal
government attempts not only to raise the tax revenue it
feels it should or must have, but it also tries to shape other
elements of our lives. Our tax code penalizes some things
and encourages others. For example, permitting taxpayers
to deduct mortgage interest tends to encourage home ownership. As another example, our progressive-rate structure
taxes higher-income people at a higher tax rate. This tends
to discourage some workers from making the effort necessary to earn more money. The trouble with this kind of
politics is that, as the politicians attempt to do one kind of
good, they can do another kind of harm.

One of the hottest topics in Congress and on radio and
TV talk shows is overhauling the entire concept of how we
pay taxes. As you have learned in this chapter, we currently
have what is called a "progressive" tax structure. Not only
do you pay more taxes if you earn more, but you pay an
even higher rate of taxes. Some people are pushing for a
"flat" tax. This would mean that everyone would pay the
same rate of tax on the income they earn. This is not a new
idea, but the flat tax idea now is being supported more

widely. There are always two sides to a story. The supporters of a flat tax claim that, not only is it inherently more fair, but that it would encourage productivity, encourage people to work harder, and encourage people to earn more. They claim that the current system is a disincentive for people to make more money. The other side claims higher-income people *should* pay disproportionately higher taxes to subsidize those who earn less. Which philosophy has more merit? Beauty is often in the eyes of the beholder!

Until changes are made, you must face the tax system currently in place. When you fill out your tax return, you must pay what the law requires. In tax payments as well as in every other aspect of life, be honest. Don't cheat!

As the old saying goes, there are two things we can be sure of in life—death and taxes!

Summary

In writing this book, we learned a lot. The meetings, the discussions, comparing notes, consulting other people for ideas, gathering information, looking up things we weren't sure about, and the discipline of organizing and doing the writing—all of these things and more taught both of us a lot.

Here were two people that saw and felt a need to make practical information about money and credit available to young adults who wanted to learn. One of us has spent his entire career teaching banking and finance; the other has devoted more than three decades to working with people who got into financial trouble, often because they didn't learn some of the things covered in this book when they were young. When this project started, we both thought we pretty much knew it all. Well, we are telling you that we didn't. Writing this book helped us realize that.

We hope you have gotten something worthwhile out of it also. We hope it is something that will stay with you through life and will reward you in the years ahead. There was a lot we couldn't cover in these pages. There is just so much to learn about life and money. In this day and age, the two have become closely connected—maybe too much so.

Not many of us live on farms anymore. We don't grow what we eat ourselves, nor do we spend much of our time on basic survival activities just to stay alive. Our economic and social structure has evolved into something that is much more complex. We do and make things for other people, and they do and make things for us. This leaves us no choice but to use a medium of exchange—money. We exchange our labor and talents for money. Then we use it to buy the things we need and, to the degree we can afford them, things we want.

Those of you who master the use of your money, that unit of measure of your labor and talent, will grow and prosper. Less of your earning power will be wasted on mistakes. More of it will be wisely invested in a better standard of living. Some people are slaves to their money. That is sad and a waste. Their money should be their slave—a tool to use wisely and treat with respect.

Credit has become indispensable in our social and economic structure. As we enter the twenty-first century, it will be even more so. There are incredible changes taking place, even as you read this, that will benefit those who build good credit and prove that they are responsible. Many of those changes are going to leave others behind, totally out of the race.

In today's market, currency is used much less than it was only a decade ago. In the next ten years, it will be used even less. Fewer and fewer employers will hand out paychecks. Your earnings will be directly deposited electronically into a financial institution. Writing checks rapidly is becoming out-dated. Credit cards and debit cards are here to stay, and even more important and exciting tools are on the way. So-called "smart cards" and "electronic money" will reduce even further the importance of checks and currency.

You will have to learn to use the new tools related to money and credit. The best of them will require proof of your responsibility—proof that you can manage your resources and your business correctly. People who can't, or won't, will be left behind.

We hope we have had a positive influence on your thinking about yourself and your role in the marketplace. Money doesn't grow on trees, and everyone cannot have everything he or she wants. You cannot expect the government to take care of you. We hope you have learned something about setting goals and going after them. Your life and your future are your responsibility. Take care of them.

So how do you manage? How do you get the things you need and want? How do you make the most of the money we make? Since there are no easy solutions, what are the answers?

Experience, learning, and the application of common sense mixed with some self-discipline are the answers. Experience takes time, but you have the opportunity to learn a lot right here in this book. Common sense is the application of experience and learning. Self-discipline is the tough part. None of us want to wait or be patient for what we want. But self-discipline is a trait that can be learned.

You have finished this book, and you haven't discovered any magic tricks. And you're not going to in life, either. We've shared with you a wealth of knowledge and experience, and there's more to come in your life. Be open to it. Go for it!

Appendix A

Federal Laws that Affect Consumers

In this section, we discuss the most important laws about credit that affect consumers. We do not go into the details or legal technicalities; rather, we give you a summary of what these laws cover. If you ever need more complete information, any public library will have it. Better yet, go to the Federal Trade Commission's web site: www.ftc.gov.

Truth In Lending

This law requires creditors to inform you of the cost of credit in terms of "**APR**," or "Annual Percentage Rate." Basically, this law is an "equalizer" and prevents a creditor from using a method of calculating interest that makes the interest rate sound lower that it actually is. Also, it requires a creditor to tell you when the interest starts. In the case of credit cards, which are a form of "open-end" credit, the law requires a creditor to tell you how the finance charges will be applied against the balance you owe. In other words, will there be a grace period? Will interest be charged against the average balance during the month, against the highest balance, or against the balance at the beginning of the cycle?

Equal Credit Opportunity Act

This law prohibits discrimination in the granting of credit on the basis of sex, race, color, marital status, religion, national origin, age, or because a person receives public assistance. Don't misunderstand this law. A creditor can "turn down" any credit application that does not meet credit criteria. Creditors simply cannot include any of the above factors in their policies or practices.

Fair Credit Billing Act

This law requires creditors, such as credit card issuers, to explain your rights if you are incorrectly charged on your credit account. The law sets forth what rights you have.

Fair Credit Reporting Act

This law gives consumers the right to know what information is being distributed by a credit bureau. It also gives a consumer rights to correct any erroneous information. The law also requires a creditor who turns down your credit application to tell you which credit bureau provided information that was used in the decision to deny credit.

Fair Debt Collection Act

This law prohibits debt collectors from violating your rights by setting forth certain things. Collectors cannot use

Appendix B

Bankruptcy

This information is in no way intended to explain the laws about bankruptcy. Instead, we discuss the practical realities of how bankruptcy affects people, the economy, and the *concept of being responsible*. We also briefly cover the different kinds of bankruptcy.

There are some people who would lead you to believe that bankruptcy is no big deal and that everybody does it. They say that big shots and major corporations go bankrupt all the time. They imply that, if you have trouble paying debts, there is no reason you should not file for bankruptcy. These things simply are not true.

In the first place, the fact that a person has filed any kind of bankruptcy will be reported by credit reporting agencies on the credit record of the debtor for seven to ten years. The result is that essential credit like that for transportation or housing is more expensive and harder to get in the future.

In addition, not many big shots or corporations go bankrupt. If this were true, our entire economic system would collapse and there would be financial chaos. It is true that a small percent get into trouble and file for protection under bankruptcy laws. Usually this is under *Chapter 11 Reorganization*, which is a special provision in bankruptcy. More on this later.

It is also not true that the majority of everyday people go bankrupt. Again, if this were a fact, there would be economic collapse. There would be no such thing as credit as we know it, because credit is based on faith and trust that people will pay their debts.

There is, however, a bankruptcy law designed to provide a fresh start for those who get into financial trouble. That is necessary. There must be some form of legal relief for people who really cannot pay their debts. Many years ago, in England, people were actually put into prison if they did not pay their debts! It was called "debtor's prison." Well, that is not done anymore. Bankruptcy is not a sugar-coated pill. It is not a cure-all. It is not a "solution" to all financial problems. It should be considered only as a *last-chance alternative* for someone in very serious financial trouble. Even if someone is in desperate trouble and filing bankruptcy becomes necessary, doing so will carry prices and penalties.

How Bankruptcy Can Affect People

Most importantly, bankruptcy is financial failure. It is not good for people to fail in anything. When they do, there is a tendency to try to justify it. To justify a failure, one must rationalize that he or she couldn't help it or that the failure could not have been avoided. This is a strong human trait, but it is not a healthy one. The very act of rationalizing one failure or mistake makes it easier to justify the next failure or mistake. All of us will encounter adversity in life. Each time we overcome that adversity, we will be the stronger for doing so. We want to build on successes, not justify failures.

We repeat that bankruptcy sometimes is unavoidable. This is often after the fact, after the mistakes are made and the damage is done. If we get into a serious auto accident and are sued for hundreds of thousands of dollars, maybe the accident could have been avoided. Or, maybe we weren't carrying enough liability insurance. Perhaps we got sick and piled up impossible medical bills. We could have taken better care of our health or had better health insurance.

There are bankruptcies where there is truly no fault of the debtor, but these may be the exception. There was no omission, nor was there anything sensible the person could have done to avoid the problem that caused the impossible amount of debt. Even then, there is still a sense of failure.

The point is that, under most circumstances, bankruptcy is not a good thing. It damages people.

How Can Someone in Trouble Avoid Bankruptcy?

There are common-sense things that a person who is tempted to consider bankruptcy first should try to fully explore:

1. Increase income. There are many ways that a well-motivated person can increase income. Lots of people work two jobs and for many reasons. One of the authors has a fine young employee (not in financial trouble) who works two jobs to save money for a down payment on a home, and another who moonlights to put two children through college.

2. Decrease living expenses. Very few people in true poverty get into too much debt. Most credit users have average and often high incomes. People with average incomes almost always can cut their living expenses a great deal if they are well motivated to do so.

3. Decrease debt. While this option is seldom a cure-all, many people who get into trouble do so because they buy too many things. There often are possessions such as a car, a boat, guns, or whatever that can be sold and the proceeds used to decrease debt. Nothing is as valuable as your reputation. Any "goods" given up to help reduce debt can be replaced later in life. Too many people place false pride in possessions.

Anyone having difficulty meeting monthly payments on time should immediately call each creditor and explain the problem. Most creditors are very helpful. But, you must take the first step and communicate.

Finally, we have told you that there are hundreds of quality conscious non-profit credit counseling companies nationwide. If you are sincere and willing to make sacrifices, most can get your creditors to cooperate with a common-sense repayment plan that will fit your budget.

How Does Bankruptcy Affect the Economy?

When someone, or a company, goes bankrupt, the debts don't magically go away. Uncle Sam doesn't pay them. The creditors who are owed must "charge off" the debts. This term means that money is lost to that business owner or the stockholders. There is a real loss, not a paper one. The only way a business can absorb a loss is to pass it on in the form of higher prices to those who do pay their bills. A business can only raise prices so much and remain competitive. If the business can no longer be competitive, it will lose its customers and go out of business.

In a recent year, more than $40,000,000,000 in consumer debt was discharged in bankruptcy. That is a staggering $40 billion! Guess who bore that burden? Those losses were passed on to every American household in increased prices for goods and services. Each household's share averaged out to an estimated $400.

There is no free lunch. We are all part of this economic system. If any part of it hurts, we are all hurt. Therefore, bankruptcy is bad for business, and it is bad for you and me.

The Kinds of Bankruptcy

The Federal Bankruptcy Act is a very complicated set of laws. We will give you only a few important highlights. But, first, we need to tell you something basic about the bankruptcy law. The Bankruptcy Judge is not there to help someone decide whether filing bankruptcy is the right thing to do. The Bankruptcy Code (the set of laws) is simply there.

The Bankruptcy Judge can only rule on questions brought before him or her about what the law says can and cannot be done. Even bankruptcy attorneys who regularly represent debtors can only advise on what the bankruptcy laws can do and what they cannot do. Ultimately, the person in financial trouble has to decide if filing bankruptcy is what they should or should not do.

Chapter 7 Bankruptcy

This is the part of the Bankruptcy Code under which most cases are filed. Its purpose is to obtain an order called a "discharge." To get the relief available under Chapter 7, a person files a petition requesting that relief and answers a series of questions about his or her personal financial affairs. During the life of the case, the person filing bankruptcy is called a Debtor. The person must also file a sworn list of all amounts owed to everyone. This affidavit must also provide the names and addresses of those to whom the debts are owed, the reasons for the debts, and a list of all property—all things of value—the person owns. The persons to whom money is owed are called the creditors. Complete disclosure of debts and property of all kinds is required. The Court then orders the creditors to stop collection efforts during the case.

The Court appoints a person called a Trustee to review the papers filed, to question the debtor about his or her finances and property, and to investigate further if necessary. The Trustee is required to recognize that certain property is exempt. Exempt property includes certain necessary things that cannot be taken away from the debtor. All property that is not exempt and that is worth the cost to sell it and get cash for it must be turned over to the Trustee. After the sale of this property, the trustee then distributes the cash obtained to the creditors. In most cases, of course, that cash does not go far, and the balance of the debts are lost to the creditors.

The Bankruptcy Court ultimately issues to the debtor a "discharge," which orders the creditors not to ever pursue collection of the debts. This does not include debts resulting from any property that was purchased but not paid for, or from property on which the debtor had agreed to give the creditor a mortgage or security interest. Where the purchase price of an item has not been paid, or a mortgage or security interest has been given, the creditor can require the debtor to either surrender that property to the creditor or pay for it, even after a discharge in a Chapter 7 case. The debtor must pay his or her attorney's fee and certain court costs.

The discharge in a Chapter 7 case generally does not prevent the collection of the following debts.

- Student loans unless a special suit is filed to prove extreme hardship

- Tax debts less than three years old

- Debts for alimony and child support

- Loans made to pay certain federal taxes

- Debts for intentional injury to people or property

- Debts for fraud including seriously misleading credit applications

- Debts owed for repayment of amounts stolen or for the value of stolen property

Chapter 13 Bankruptcy

The purpose of this kind of bankruptcy is to propose a plan for the repayment of at least some of the debtor's debts under the protection of the Bankruptcy Court. As in a Chapter 7 case, the debtor must first file a petition and the lists of debts and property. The Court then orders the creditors to stop collection efforts during the case. The Court appoints a trustee to review the papers filed, to question the debtor about his or her finances and property, and to investigate further if necessary. The debtor must propose a plan for the repayment of most tax debts and child support debts, and to pay at least the value of any mortgaged property. The plan must also pay to the rest of the creditors at least as much as they would have been paid in a Chapter 7 case after assets were sold. A corporation may not file under Chapter 13.

If these and other requirements are met, and if the debtor has enough regular monthly income to make the planned payments, the Court will force the creditors to go along with the repayment plan. Such Chapter 13 plans are often used to allow a debtor to keep some kinds of property and pay for it over time. Plans are usually three years long but may last up to five years. The plan usually will require that the debtor's employer take most of the money called for by the plan out of the debtor's wages and pay it directly to the trustee, who then pays the money to the creditors. The debtor must pay his or her attorney's fee and certain court costs. In addition, the trustee retains up to ten percent of the amount of money paid from the debtor's wages as a fee for reviewing the papers and handling the money.

At the end of the Chapter 13 plan, the Court issues a discharge order for any portion of the debts not paid in the plan. The discharge in a Chapter 13 case generally does not prevent the collection of the following debts.

- Student loans unless there is a special suit filed to prove extreme hardship
- Tax debts less than three years old
- Debts for alimony and child support
- Debts for injuries caused by driving while intoxicated
- Debts owed for repayment of amounts stolen or for the value of stolen property

In about two-thirds of Chapter 13 cases, the debtor is unable or unwilling to complete the plan payments. When that happens, the Chapter 13 case is dismissed or is converted to a Chapter 7 case. A dismissal leaves the debtor to deal with his original debts and the amounts that have been further delayed during the Chapter 13 case. This can be a worse situation than before filing the Chapter 13 case. If the case is converted to Chapter 7, then the trustee will sell off the available assets to pay the creditors.

Chapter 11

Bankruptcy cases filed under this Chapter also require the filing of a plan. This plan is not for typical consumers, although it can apply to a few. The purpose of Chapter 11 is to give a company (or the individual) in financial trouble a chance to reorganize its finances. The goal is to become profitable again and save the company. Some Chapter 11s are successful, and the company later thrives. Others are not successful and fall into Chapter 7.

When you hear of a company filing for bankruptcy, it is often filing a Chapter 11 reorganization. In a Chapter 11 reorganization, a company is afforded an immediate reprieve from creditors. It must, within a certain time period, file a plan to reorganize with the Bankruptcy Court. This plan must be very comprehensive. It must spell out exactly how the company proposes to deal with its debts and obligations and how it proposes to operate while under the protection of the Court. A trustee is not usually appointed, and often the Court has much to say about what the company can and cannot do in running its business during the reorganization. The creditors have certain rights in the proceedings. If a plan is approved, then the company may operate within that plan in its efforts to become a solvent company again.

Chapter 12 and Other Chapters

Chapter 12 is a special part of the bankruptcy law designed exclusively for family farmers. There are other chapters for railroads, stockbrokers, and a few other special cases.

Food for Thought

Creditors agree that there must be some form of a bankruptcy law. Creditors agree that even prudent and responsible people can (but rarely) find themselves saddled with an impossible amount of debt. A serious health problem, disability, or accident can wipe out a person financially. Then, too, an extended period of unemployment on top of heavy debt can bring hardship—even for someone who may have had savings.

Many people feel that the present bankruptcy laws do not constructively address the need. These laws originated many years ago when nearly all credit was heavily secured with collateral. Times have changed. Credit today is primarily extended on faith, trust, and the promise to repay out of future income—even when there is collateral. While many bankruptcies today cannot be avoided, there is growing concern that too many people use bankruptcy as an easy way out of debts that they made to purchase goods and services. There is also a concern that too many people who file a bankruptcy case do so under Chapter 7 and just walk away from their debts when they would be able to pay at least some of their debts. Therefore, if they file for bankruptcy relief, they should do so under Chapter 13.

Although this Appendix is about bankruptcy, this is a good place to mention the subject of civil lawsuits filed to collect a debt. Creditors do not want to sue people for nonpayment. But when other attempts to collect fail, they must strive to collect the money that is owed them. When you sign a note or other agreement, it will say that if the debt is placed in the hands of an attorney for collection, you agree to pay court costs, attorney's fees, and interest. The following is a factual example of how much extra the debtor will pay if an attorney has to collect the debt. The amount owed when the debtor defaulted was $1,756.57. It took 434 days to collect the debt by suit and garnishment of wages. By the time interest, court costs, sheriff's commissions, and attorney fees were added, the debtor paid a total of $3,090.50. The moral of this story? Use credit wisely, pay your bills on time, and don't get sued!

According to Webster

Bankrupt (noun): 1a: a person who has done any of the acts that by law entitle his creditors to have his estate administered for their benefit **b:** a person judicially declared subject to having his estate administered under the bankrupt laws for the benefit of his creditors **c:** a person who becomes insolvent **2:** one who is destitute of a particular thing <a moral *bankrupt*>

Bankrupt (adj): 1a: reduced to a state of financial ruin: IMPOVERISHED; *specifically* : legally declared a bankrupt <the company went *bankrupt*> **b:** of or relating to bankrupts or bankruptcy <*bankrupt* laws> **2a:** BROKEN, RUINED <a *bankrupt* professional career> **b:** exhausted of valuable qualities : STERILE <a bankrupt old culture> **c:** DESTITUTE—used with *of* or *in* <*bankrupt* of all merciful feelings>

Bankruptcy (noun): 1: the quality or state of being bankrupt **2:** utter failure or impoverishment.

Source: *Merriam Webster's Collegiate ® Dictionary, Tenth Edition.*

Appendix C

Non-Profit Credit Counseling Services

There was a time when, if a person got too deep into debt, there was no place to turn except to the lawyers and the Bankruptcy Court. That time was before the concept of non-profit credit counseling came to life over 40 years ago. Today, there is face-to-face, non-profit help available to nearly everyone in the country. Most of these offices are named Consumer Credit Counseling Services, but many operate under different names. For people who have no office nearby, toll-free telephone counseling is available. This CCCS provides telephone counseling and can be reached at 1-800-364-5595.

The publisher of this book is Credit Counseling Services of Louisiana, Inc., which operates 16 offices in Louisiana and Arkansas under the name Consumer Credit Counseling Services.

You should always check out a company before you do important business with it. The same applies here. Were you or someone you know ever to need the services of a credit counseling company, you should check it out. A good

way is to find out if it is a member of the National Foundation for Credit Counseling. Simply ask, and look for the
NFCC seal. Members of the NFCC must meet stringent standards, far too many to list here! There may be legitimate
companies other than NFCC members, but we do not know
how you would check them out to be sure you should do
business with them.

Look for the NFCC seal

There are nearly 200 autonomous members of the NFCC
that operate over 1,300 offices across the country. Autonomous means that each is a separate corporation with its
own board of directors. All share a common mission: money
management and credit counseling, Debt Repayment Programs for those with serious financial problems, and educational programs teaching and promoting the responsible
use of credit. Again, most are named CCCS, but all will
display the NFCC seal.

These non-profit companies are able to play a beneficial
role because:

- Most people who experience financial difficulty are
  honest and want to repay their debts. Thank goodness!

- The creditors they owe are responsible business
  people. They much prefer to see their customers get
  help, and will both cooperate with and financially
  support non-profit counseling services.

- These services are independent, neutral third-parties,
  and thus are able to work with all concerned to reach
  common goals.

Even though most people seen by these services are financially over-obligated, they have incomes and are not destitute. Although they may be in trouble, there is usually income to work with. By tailoring and administering a realistic, disciplined budget and obtaining the cooperation of creditors, the debts can be repaid.

How Are These Companies Governed?

These services are governed by local boards of directors made up from all segments of the community. Their directors are leading citizens and business people active in community affairs. These men and women serve without compensation. Their role is to set policy, direction, and goals. A board employs a president or executive director who is charged with carrying out the mission of the service. This chief executive is responsible for managing the affairs of the program and staffing the agency with counselors and the many other employees who are necessary for the agency to deliver its services.

How Are These Companies Funded?

Non-profit agencies must have income with which to operate, just as any other business must have. That income must exceed expenses so that they may have operating capital. The majority of income of these services comes from responsible creditors who know that even an honest customer may one day encounter financial difficulties. Quite naturally, businesses want these customers to be able to get help so they can pay their bills. Perhaps even more important, most businesses truly want to help for humanitarian reasons. It's good for the community, for the economy, for all concerned. We have already told you that the alternative, bankruptcy, is bad for everyone.

Most services have small user fees in one form or another. With some there may be a small cost for initial counseling, although most of these companies never charge for this help. If the problems are serious and a Debt Repayment Plan is needed, most services will have a small fee to help defray the costs of administering a plan. We cover the Debt Repayment Plan later.

Some services are a part of United Way and get some of their income from that source. There can be other sources of income, depending upon the community in which the service is established. But, business creditors contribute the majority of income.

What Services Can These Companies Provide?

The most important services provided are counseling, educational programs and, where necessary, a Debt Repayment Plan for someone in serious trouble.

Counseling alone, with no further involvement by the agency, can help many people in financial trouble. But in other cases, there may be obstacles that the client cannot overcome alone. The client may need the counseling service to contact creditors and arrange a plan to make payments within his or her means. This is known as a Debt Repayment Plan. In a DRP, the client will make a single monthly payment to the agency. The agency then will disburse payments each month to the creditors in accordance with the plan.

These agencies provide many educational services. They include not only counseling to individual clients, but programs for the general public. These programs take a variety of forms, usually including seminars, distribution of information on budgeting and the wise use of credit, and sometimes classes taught in schools. Seminars offered may cover a variety of topics ranging from classes on budgeting to first-time homebuyer programs. Clients who go through a Debt Repayment Program may receive the best financial education in the world—actually living the experience of making a budget work. These clients who make the program work for them rarely get into trouble again!

How Can Someone in Need Get Counseling?

In most cases, help is but a phone call away. Nearly every service in the country is easily accessible and strives to give appointments for counseling very quickly. Procedures may vary slightly, but the first thing for someone to do is pick up the phone and call the nearest service. In larger communities, look in the white pages under Consumer Credit Counseling Service. If this doesn't do the trick, call the Better Business Bureau if one is in your area, or call one of the larger creditors you may owe. You may also look in the Yellow Pages under "credit and debt counseling," but caution is urged here. As we have previously advised, check out any unknown agency. When you contact a program in your area, a representative will answer your questions about getting an appointment. And, as we have said, telephone counseling is available no matter where you live. Another excellent way to get help is through the Internet. The web site of this CCCS is www.realhelp.org. Information there explains the program, and forms may be completed online and submitted via secure server.

A realistic note here. In serious cases, there is no easy solution. Excessive debt, often accumulated over a period of years, will not magically go away. Sincere people who wish to overcome too much debt may have to make sensible sacrifices to live within a budget while repaying their debts. But only through meeting adversity head on and overcoming it can any of us build our strengths. No one gets through this life without bumps and bruises, and all too often they involve money. Every time we meet a challenge and overcome it, we are stronger and better for it. If, on the other hand, we make excuses to justify a failure, we become prone to making the same mistakes again and again.

Appendix D

Better Business Bureaus

BBBs, like Consumer Credit Counseling Services, are non-profit community service organizations. Their boards function much the same as in the case of CCCS programs, serving without compensation.

A BBB is sponsored by private business and is dedicated to the public interest serving business, consumers, and the marketplace.

What Services does a BBB Provide?

A BBB provides a variety of services to the public and also to businesses. Among them are the following.

Inquiries

A consumer, or a business, wishing to check the background of someone he or she is considering doing business with, may telephone the local BBB for a report. This report will provide background information on a business as well as its track record regarding customer complaints. This information really can help a consumer avoid a possibly unhappy experience if he or she will call the BBB *before* doing business with an unknown firm.

The BBB also provides reports on organizations that solicit donations.

If you call inquiring about a company that is not on file with the BBB, the BBB will try to develop a report or refer you to another BBB that may have information.

Complaints

The BBB has experienced personnel who can assist with advice or consumer-related complaints. A BBB will require that you put a complaint in writing. Only in that way can the organization act on it. When a complaint is filed, the BBB will immediately contact the business involved. Every effort will be made to resolve the dispute. This process may take only a few days or up to several weeks. Even the most responsible business is, sooner or later, going to displease a customer. When this occurs, the business usually is very cooperative with a BBB in resolving things to everyone's satisfaction.

Arbitration

The Better Business Bureau administers an arbitration program. This procedure is often successful in resolving a dispute that could not be handled by normal procedures.

In these cases, trained volunteer arbitrators conduct a hearing and render a decision that is binding on each party who has agreed to the arbitration. Many national companies have standing agreements with BBBs to be willing to arbitrate any dispute.

Arbitration is an excellent program. It offers a means to resolve problems without involving lawyers and courts.

Advertising Review

The BBB has an ongoing program of monitoring advertising. This is a means of helping to maintain accuracy and honesty in advertising. Whenever an ad appears to be deceptive or misleading or not in compliance with advertising codes, the BBB will contact the advertiser. The purpose is to assist an honest merchant to make any appropriate changes. This is a voluntary, self-regulation program.

Membership

A BBB is financially supported by business firms that meet and maintain certain standards. All firms are pre-screened before being invited to be a member of the BBB. All applications for membership in the BBB must be approved by the BBB's board of directors.

The more a BBB is used by the public, the better its services are! Any consumer feeling he or she has a valid complaint with a business firm should call the BBB. The BBB may be able to solve the problem for the consumer. If it is a legitimate complaint and the merchant will not attempt to correct the problem, the complaint is filed and reported to the next consumer inquiring about that business. In this way, the BBB builds a favorable file on businesses that serve the public fairly, and builds a complaint file on those that are not responsive.

For more information on Better Business Bureaus, go to their national web site at www.bbb.org.

Appendix E

Gambling—Recreation or Addiction?

Gambling is mentioned in this book for two reasons. First, gambling is so much more accessible today to so many more people. Second, gambling can have a devastating impact on one's financial life.

A few short years ago, if you wanted to gamble, you had to go to Las Vegas or to one of the very few other places in America where gambling was legal. That has changed—lotteries, video poker machines, and casinos have sprung up across the United States.

Our purpose here is not moralistic. We are not going to try to convince you that gambling is evil or wrong. Gambling has been around as long as dirt. Like a lot of other things in life, if taken in moderation, gambling may not hurt you. Our purpose is to simply to arm you with information.

Experience has proven that some people cannot deal with any form of gambling, even in small doses. For those people, it quickly becomes an addictive compulsion. When that happens, it rapidly dominates and destroys their lives.

Also, gambling often hurts the lives of the family members of compulsive gamblers.

The same thing happens with alcohol. Most people can take an occasional drink and leave it alone the rest of the time. Others must practice complete abstinence or alcohol will overwhelm them.

Gambling will hurt you financially because the deck is stacked against you! In any form of commercial gambling, you are not supposed to win. The games, and the mathematical odds, are carefully controlled so that you will lose. Otherwise, the people who own the gambling enterprises would lose. Out of every dollar that is gambled, a certain amount must go to pay for overhead (the expenses of the facility, salaries, and so on), a certain amount for taxes, and another amount for profit to the owners. That does not leave much to be returned to the players in the form of winnings! If you are of legal age and your budget can afford a few recreational dollars, then that's another matter. Spend those recreation dollars however you choose. Just understand that, if you try to gamble with anything other than recreation in mind, you will lose more than your budget can stand.

Gambling is a multi-billion-dollar industry. Owners of casinos, riverboats, video poker machines, and other gambling facilities are not taking chances. They are in control of the odds—you are not. They are after profits, and these profits must come from the players.

Again, we are not preaching morality—just reality. The chances of you winning big bucks are close to zero. Even the highly publicized state lotteries are, in the words of a well-known, self-admitted gambler, "a sucker's bet."

We could fill this book with facts on gambling—odds, numbers, you name it. To give you but a small glimpse of what is going on, we will state just one example. In Louisiana alone, the "take" in a recent 12-month period was *two billion dollars!* The "take" is not the amount of money bet, *but the amount lost!* And, that does not include the money bet and lost at the several Indian-owned casinos, as they are not required to report data.

Appendix F

Your Vote, Your Voice—Make It Heard

This book is about you and how you can make yourself better financially. We cover things that affect your pocketbook. You've read about taxes—how the government takes and spends a part of your earnings. So, you will want to have a voice in government. You will want to affect how government taxes and spends. In other words, you will want to vote.

If you are not yet 18, you will be before you know it. At one time in America, you had to be 21 before you got the right to vote. You could go to war to defend your freedom before you could vote. Back then, a great majority of kids looked forward to when they could vote. It represented an achievement, or rite of passage, so to speak. We wonder if that's true any more. Voting records tell us that there has been a disturbing trend in the past generation, with fewer and fewer people exercising their right to vote. Fewer still communicate their views on proposed laws to their representatives.

If that dangerous trend continues, fewer people will be deciding the future of this great country. As politicians learn that people no longer take an active role in what laws are passed, they will take greater liberties in deciding what they think is best for you. That is harmful to the idea of personal freedom. Politicians will be more and more accountable to the fewer people that do vote—and less accountable to the people who don't vote. That is dangerous.

That trend must be reversed if this country is to continue in its tradition as the greatest country in the world. What do you think has made us the greatest country in the world? Our people, our form of government, and our right to vote.

The voting trend can be reversed—but only starting with you. So, if or when you are 18, vote. If you don't know who to vote for, or even what you would be voting about, ask other people. Ask your relatives, your friends, your employer—anyone you look up to. Read, read, and read. Take a position. Find out what each politician, or each candidate for office, stands for. Then, take your position and vote. Your vote does not have to be a correct one by anyone else's opinion. That is the beauty of our system.

If you do not vote, you have lost your voice.

By the way, if you don't think this is such a great country, then can you tell us why most of the rest of the world would love to come here?

Appendix G

Internet Resources

www.cccs-RealHelp.org

Visit our web site to learn all about CCCS and the services we offer. Visit our "Consumer Educational Tips" page to learn about the wise use of credit and budgeting, and you can also download Excel spreadsheets containing our consumer budgeting forms. Our "CCCS In Action" page addresses a new topic from time to time relative to educational and community projects in which we're involved. Also, visit our "Links" page for links to some of our favorite consumer-oriented sites.

www.zillions.org

Zillions Online is supported by Consumers Union, the nonprofit publisher of "Consumer Reports." The web site exists to motivate and prepare kids to make informed and independent consumer decisions, and to develop consumer literacy that will serve them and society throughout their lives.

www.taxweb.com

This is the Internet's first consumer-oriented source for federal, state, and local tax-related developments. It contains a wealth of links to tax-related sites.

www.equifax.com
www.experian.com
www.transunion.com

Visit the web sites of the three major credit reporting agencies to learn about credit reporting or to order a copy of your credit report online.

www.consumerworld.org

Consumer World® is a public service site that has gathered over 2,000 of the most useful consumer resources on the Internet, and categorized them on their web site for easy access. Whether you want to find buying advice and product reviews, comparison shop for bargains and last minute travel, file a consumer complaint with a government or company consumer affairs department or the BBB, read 100s of consumer rights booklets, find a low rate credit card or mortgage, look up the wholesale price of a car, get personal finance tips, read news of the latest scams, research a law, clip electronic coupons, or search the Internet, you can do it in Consumer World.

www.stretcher.com

This site contains the weekly newsletter, "The Dollar Stretcher—Living Better for Less." It is a weekly resource for better living and offers thousands of tips on ways to save money and live more economically. This is an excellent site to research tips for saving money on just about anything!

www.ftc.gov

The Federal Trade Commission offers a wealth of information to consumers. "ConsumerLine" is the online service of the Office of Consumer and Business Education of the Bureau of Consumer Protection. This site offers information on consumer protection, business guidance, formal actions, opinions, activities, and much more. The

Consumer Protection section of the site offers many publications and education campaigns designed with the consumer in mind.

The Federal Trade Commission enforces a variety of federal antitrust and consumer protection laws.

www.consumer.gov

The *U.S. Consumer Gateway*—"consumer.gov"—is a "one-stop" link to a broad range of federal information resources available online. It is designed so that you can locate information by category—such as Food, Health, Product Safety, Your Money, and Transportation. Each category has subcategories to direct you to areas within individual federal web sites containing related information. This site is brought to you by the Federal Trade Commission and a wealth of other federal agencies such as the Centers for Disease Control, the Department of Education, the Department of Veterans Affairs, the Federal Communications Commission, the National Park Service, the U.S. Consumer Product Safety Commission, the U.S. Postal Service, and many others.

www.pueblo.gsa.gov

This site is offered by the Federal Consumer Information Center in Pueblo, CO. View, search, and order full-text versions of hundreds of consumer-oriented publications along with the latest edition of the Consumer's Resource Handbook. Categories of their publications include Cars, Children, Employment, Federal Programs, Food & Nutrition, Health, Housing, Money, Small Business, Travel, and Miscellaneous.

www.financenter.com/calculate/all_calculate.fs

FinanCenter.com is a profitable, independent, privately-held Internet company established in 1995. As a consumer advocate in all areas of personal finance, FinanCenter.com publishes research on rates, fees, features, and customer satisfaction levels for financial products and services online. This link will bring you to the site's award-winning Web calculators that compute borrowing, investing, and spending options to help consumers understand and find the best options when making financial decisions.

www.fraud.org

This site is brought to you by the National Fraud Information Center, a project of the National Consumers League. The NFIC's award-winning web site not only enables consumers to get answers to their questions and report possible fraud, but it is a valuable educational tool. Check out their News & Views section, the Internet Fraud Watch section, the telemarketing tips, the special elder fraud information, and other features.

www.usnews.com/usnews/nycu/money/mohome.htm

U.S. News Online "News You Can Use" contains some great information on money, including information on setting up a personal budget and setting up a savings plan. You can also test out their money toolbox, which contains loads of calculators with which you can get information on mutual funds, credit and credit cards, retirement, refinancing, and interest rates. One of the savings calculators even tells you what it will take to become a millionaire!

www.money.com/money

Money Magazine's "Financial Strategy Center" offers of wealth of information on markets and market news, investing, real estate, insurance, small business, and many other money-related topics. Take the interactive "Money 101" course on budgeting and planning, investing, and insurance. Take a look at some lessons on investing basics, buying a home, understanding insurance, how to buy a car, and many others.

www.cnnfn.com
www.quicken.com/banking and credit
www.bankrate.com

These are also some excellent sites offering investment and financial news and information, calculators, competitive rates on cards and loan products, newsletters, and much more.

www.ncfe.org

The National Center for Financial Education's web site offers some great financial lessons for consumers, including "Don't Be a Debt-Head," "Credit File Correction," "Money Helps," "Tips for Using Credit and Credit Cards," and "Children and Money."

www.credit-info.com

This site offers some good information for consumers about credit reports, dealing with creditors and bill collectors, consumer protection, and many other topics. New to the site is its consumer protection database of state banking regulators, Better Business Bureaus, and consumer protection agencies.

www.wa.gov/ago/youth

The Washington State Attorney General's Office web site hosts an excellent section on consumer education for teens. In fact, it was written by teens, for teens with the intent to help teenagers (a group commonly targeted by businesses and scam artists) become educated consumers. The site offers helpful consumer tips and topics of great interest to teenagers, including music clubs, apartment renting, college scholarship and Internet scams, health clubs, car buying, and even tatoos!

www.wisepockets.com

This site is a great place for kids, parents, and teachers to learn about managing money. The site was produced by the Center for Entrepeneurship and Economic Education at the University of Missouri–St.Louis and is based on the National Center for Economic Education's K-12 Financial Economics Program. If you have younger brothers, sisters, or other relatives, have some fun introducing them to the world of money by taking them on a visit to this web site. Let them join the "Wise Pockets Clubhouse for Kids" and take part in interactive lessons on making, spending, and saving money.

www.thinkquest.org

"ThinkQuest" is an educational initiative committed to advancing learning through the use of computer and network technology. This site challenges teachers and students of all ages to use the Internet in innovative and exciting ways as a collaborative, interactive teaching and learning tool. Each ThinkQuest program encourages participants to create high quality, content rich, educational web sites that are made available freely to others around the world. ThinkQuest programs include the ThinkQuest Internet Challenge, ThinkQuest Junior, and Tomorrow's Teachers, among others.

Appendix H

Glossary

ATM—An automated teller machine which accepts deposits and allows withdrawals from accounts at depository institutions.

Annual Percentage Rate—The interest rate on loans calculated uniformly as provided in the Truth in Lending Act so that borrowers can compare interest rates charged by different lenders.

Assets—What a person owns.

Assigned Risk—Individuals who have a bad driving record in terms of tickets and accidents and who cannot get regular insurance are put into an assigned risk pool, and insurance is provided at high premiums.

Availability of Funds—The delay which a depository institution may impose on your access to funds after you have deposited checks drawn against another depository institution.

Balance Sheet—A snapshot of a person's financial condition as of a certain date. It shows a person's assets, liabilities, and net worth.

Balancing the Checkbook—The process of proving that the individual depositor's records agree with the bank statement.

Borrower—One who gives a promise to repay in a credit transaction. (See Debtor)

Borrowing Money—A way to get money by exchanging a promise to repay in the future.

Capacity—In terms of credit, a person's ability to borrow and repay money as determined by his or her disposable income.

Capital—Tools, equipment, factories, and the like which workers need to produce goods and services. Capital is one of the factors of production.

Capital Gains—An increase in the market value of a corporation stock which a person owns. As the market price of a stock goes up, the owner can have capital gains if he or she sells the stock at a price higher than he or she paid for it.

Car Insurance—Insurance policies which insure some of the risks involved in owning and operating an automobile.

Character—A person's reputation for being reliable, ethical, and dependable.

Checking Account—An account at a depository institution which can be used as a convenient payments mechanism.

Choices—Because not everyone can have everything that he or she wants nor do everything that he or she would like, each of us must make choices. We must choose the things or activities that we can attain from a large number of possible things or activities.

Collateral—Something of value, such as a car, a home, or savings, pledged as security on a loan.

Collision and Comprehensive—A type of automobile insurance that pays for damage to your car by vandalism, fire, or theft.

Collision Insurance—An insurance policy that pays to fix your car if you have a wreck whether or not it is your fault.

Co-maker—A co-signer. (See Co-signing)

Commercial Bank—A type of depository institution which offers to the public a broad array of services, including loans and deposits and other financial services.

Consumer Credit Counseling Service—A non-profit community service organization which helps people deal with credit problems. The service is available in all major cities in Louisiana and throughout the United States.

Consumer Finance Company—A type of entrepreneurial financial institution which specializes in small loans to individuals who may not be able to get credit at depository institutions.

Contractual Financial Institutions—People make payments to these institutions over a period of time and can get their money out only when a particular event, such as retirement or death, occurs.

Co-signing—The act of promising to repay another person's debt if that person will not or cannot repay.

Credit—Granting of money or something else of value in exchange for a promise to repay at some time in the future.

Credit Application—A form on which a potential borrower provides important information to a potential lender.

Credit Bureau—A company that gathers information on people who use credit and sells that information to companies that grant credit.

Credit Capacity—The total amount of credit which an individual or business firm can expect to have based primarily on the borrower's character, capacity, and capital.

Credit Cards—Plastic cards through which a financial institution substitutes its credit for that of the card holder, which enables the card holder to buy goods and services on credit.

Credit Life Insurance—An insurance policy which repays loans should the borrower die or become disabled.

Credit Report—The information which credit bureaus sell to companies that grant credit.

Credit Union—A depository financial institution which is owned by the members. Credit unions offer a wide array of loans and deposit products and other financial services.

Creditor—One who extends credit.

Debit Card—A card used like a credit card to make a purchase, except that the purchase price is immediately deducted from the user's checking account balance; like an electronic check.

Debtor—One who gives a promise to repay. (See Borrower)

Deductible—In insurance, a specified amount of damages or claim which must be exceeded before the insurance company pays. The insurance company pays the amount above the deductible.

Dependent—In tax terminology, someone who qualifies to be claimed on your tax return for an "Exemption," allowing a specified amount to be subtracted from taxable income. There are many rules governing who may be claimed as a dependant.

Depository Financial Institutions—Institutions in which a person deposits money and can withdraw it upon demand.

Disclosure Statement—A form which shows the borrower all costs of the transaction, including interest rate.

Disposable Income—Income which is neither needed to meet living expenses nor already committed for other debt.

Dividends—Profit distributions by corporations to shareholders who own stock in the corporations.

Down Payment—Some of the borrower's own money which, along with money borrowed from a lender, is used to buy a good, such as a house or a car.

Earned Income Credit—A special provision in federal income tax law that can actually pay money, to qualifying persons, even though no taxes were paid or due.

Earning Money—One of the ways a person gets money is earning it through providing labor in a job.

Endorsements—The process of signing the back of a check to make another individual the payee.

Endorser—One who co-signs a note or extends his or her credit to repay the loan of another if that borrower cannot or will not repay. (See Co-signing)

Entrepreneurial Financial Institutions—Companies which borrow money elsewhere and lend it to individuals.

Entrepreneurship—The creative act of putting together the five factors of production to produce goods and services.

Equity—The difference between what a person owns as of a given date and what that person owes. (See Net Worth.)

Exemption—In tax terminology, a deduction (of an amount) from taxable income for yourself and each eligible dependent.

Factors of Production—Five types of things (land, labor, capital, resources, and technology) which are required to produce every good and service.

Fair Credit Reporting Act—A federal law giving individuals the right to find out what is contained in their credit report at credit bureaus, and a procedure to correct any erroneous information.

Form 1040EZ—A federal tax form. The shortest, simplest form of all. Can be used only by a single taxpayer with no dependents.

Form 1040A—A federal tax form. For use by a taxpayer who has an income under $50,000 and does not itemize deductions.

Form 1040—A federal tax form for use by anyone who cannot file a 1040EZ or 1040A. The most complicated form.

Form 1099—A federal tax form, somewhat similar to a W-2 in purpose. It is used to report income from sources other than wages. An example is interest; a savings institution must send you a 1099 at the end of the year disclosing interest paid to you.

Functions of Money—Money serves as a medium of exchange that can be used to buy goods and services. Money also serves as a store of value in that it allows people to buy things at some time in the future. It also serves as a measure of value.

Goals—Desirable and worthwhile objectives which we seek to attain or accomplish.

Having Good Credit—The ability of a person to borrow readily.

Head of Household—A special tax filing status, qualifying eligible single persons for a lower tax rate.

Health Insurance—A type of insurance that pays, according to the terms of the policy, for medical and/or hospitalization costs.

Health and Accident Insurance—Not to be confused with true, broad coverage Health Insurance. This coverage is usually very limited and pays specific limited amounts for events specified in the policy.

Income Tax—A type of tax on the income of individuals. In the U.S., often the largest amount of tax paid by individuals, except for those who have low incomes. Imposed by the federal government and many states.

Income Tax Rate—A percentage applied against taxable income to determine taxes owed. The rate varies according to income levels.

Inflation—When there is too much money in the economy and this money is used by people to attempt to buy a limited supply of goods and services. That condition results in higher prices. Increasing prices is called inflation.

Installment Loan—A loan which the borrower pays back in periodic, usually monthly, payments.

Insurance Discounts—The discounted (reduced) premium on automobile insurance for a variety of reasons, such as being a good driver, being a good student, having taken drivers education, and the like.

Interest—The price of credit. Interest is compensation to lenders paid by borrowers.

Interest Rates—The amount of interest expressed as a percentage of the amount of money being borrowed.

Internal Revenue Service—The branch of the federal government charged with the responsibility for collecting income tax. Abbreviated "IRS."

Insurance—The process of transferring risk to others by buying a policy.

Labor—People's work or effort in the productive process. Labor is one of the factors of production.

Land—The geographical space which is required for the production of every good or service. Land is one of the factors of production.

Law of Demand—The economic principle that people buy more as the price of a good or service goes down. As the price of a good or service goes up, people buy less.

Liability Insurance—Insurance that pays for injuries or damage you may cause.

Liabilities—What a person owes.

Life Insurance—Policies which pay upon the death of the insured or, in some instances, the occasion of other events.

Life Insurance Company—A type of contractual financial institution to which a policy holder makes payments and gets his or her money out upon the occurrence of some event such as death.

Limits of Liability—An insurance term. The maximum amount(s) the insurance company is obligated to pay for damages you cause.

Luxuries of Life—Goods and services such as a diamond ring or membership in a health club which are nice to have but are not required for existence.

Market—The way people behave in an economic way. The term also means a place where buying and selling take place.

Maturity—The length of a loan.

Measure of Value—A function of money by which we gauge the relative differences between things such as incomes, prices, and wealth.

Medical Payments Coverage—This part of an insurance policy covers you and anyone in your car for medical payments up to set limits.

Medium of Exchange—A function of money by which people use money to buy goods and services.

Money—Anything which is generally accepted as a medium of exchange or a store of value is money.

Money—How You Get It—Money can be earned, borrowed, or received as a gift.

Money Market Mutual Funds—A relatively new depository financial institution which invests a saver's funds in short-term market securities.

NSF Check—When a person writing a check does not have sufficient funds in his or her checking account to cover the amount of the check.

Necessities of Life—Goods and services such as food, shelter, clothes, and medical care which are required for existence.

Net Worth—The difference between what a person owns as of a given date and what that person owes. (See Equity)

Outstanding Check—A check which has been written but has not yet been paid against the account by the depository institution.

Overdraft—A negative balance in a checking account caused by a person who writes a check for which there is not enough money in the account.

Pension Funds—A contractual financial institution to which savers make periodic deposits and get the money out upon the occasion of retirement, death, or some other event.

Price—The value of any good or service (including labor) which is determined in the marketplace.

Production—The process of combining factors of production to produce goods and services.

Progressive Income Tax Rates—As a person's taxable income increases, the additional taxable income is subject to higher federal tax rates.

Property Insurance—Often referred to as a "Homeowner's Policy." This insurance affords protection against fire, theft, storm damages, and the like. Includes liability insurance for the homeowner as well.

Reconciling Item—An item, usually something like a service charge or charge for printed checks, which must be taken into account when balancing the checkbook.

Residential Insurance—Insurance which offers protection to people who own their own homes or rent apartments or homes.

Resources—Natural things such as wood, oil, iron, or hydrogen which are required in the production of every good or service. Resources represent a factor of production.

Return on Savings—A way of earning money by investing money in order to receive interest.

Savings and Loan Associations—Depository financial institutions which primarily provide credit for purchasing homes. They offer other financial products as well.

Scarcity—Factors of production are limited, and only a limited volume of goods and services can be produced in any society. There is scarcity because everything is not available in unlimited supplies.

Social Security Tax—A federal tax on earnings, deducted from wages by an employer and paid to the government. For 1995, the rate paid by workers is 7.65 percent on the first $61,200 of earnings. This same tax amount must be matched and paid by employers.

Standard Deduction—A tax term. All taxpayers are entitled to this deduction. The amount varies according to filing status and can vary by tax year.

Store of Value—A function of money which allows people to buy things in the future.

Tax Credit—Not to be confused with a tax deduction. A credit is an amount that can be subtracted directly from taxes due.

Tax Liability—In federal income taxes, the total amount of tax owed for the year, whether this amount was withheld from earnings or not.

Tax Return—A form, either federal or state, containing information that must be reported to the government. Used to compute any tax owed, and covers a specific tax period—usually a calendar year.

Tax Withholding—An amount, determined by the W-4 form completed by an employee, that is held out of a paycheck. If the W-4 is accurately completed, the employer will hold out an amount of tax that will closely match the employee's tax liability for the year.

Taxable Income—The amount of income upon which tax must be paid. The amount after all allowances for deductions and exemptions.

Technology—Knowledge or know-how required to produce every good or service. Technology is one of the factors of production.

Term Insurance—The simplest and cheapest of life insurance policies which provides protection against death only and does not build up cash value.

Term Loan—A loan which the borrower pays back in full all at once at the end of an agreed time.

Transit Item—A deposit which a person has made but which has not yet been posted to his or her bank account.

Uninsured Motorists Insurance—A part of an automobile policy which covers injuries to you and your passengers caused by another driver who does not have insurance.

W-2—A form that an employer must send to each employee reporting earnings and tax information for the prior year. This form is necessary for completing a tax return.

W-4—A form that an employee must complete and furnish his or her employer. The information tells the employer how much federal income tax to withhold each payday. An employee can fill out a new W-4 for the employer to use anytime the employee's tax circumstances change.

Wages—The price of labor.

Whole Life Insurance—A type of life insurance which provides death benefits and which builds up "cash value" over the life of the policy.

Index